FINDING THE FIRST GREEKS OF SANTA FE
1914–1955

A WALKING TOUR OF DOWNTOWN SANTA FE

FINDING THE FIRST GREEKS OF SANTA FE

1914–1955

A WALKING TOUR OF DOWNTOWN SANTA FE

Katherine M. Pomonis
with
Yorgos D. Marinakis

Santa Fe

Sunstone books may be purchased for educational, business, or sales promotional use.
For information please write: Special Markets Department, Sunstone Press,
P.O. Box 2321, Santa Fe, New Mexico 87504-2321.
Printed on acid-free paper

Library of Congress Cataloging-in-Publication Data

Names: Pomonis, Katherine M., 1936- author. | Marinakis, Yorgos D. 1963- author.
Title: Finding the first Greeks of Santa Fe, New Mexico 1914-1955 : a walking tour of downtown Santa Fe / Katherine M. Pomonis with Yorgos D. Marinakis.
Description: Santa Fe, NM : Sunstone Press, [2024] | Summary: "A history of the Greek community in Santa Fe, New Mexico from 1914 to 1955"-- Provided by publisher.
Identifiers: LCCN 2024022262 | ISBN 9781632936752 (paperback)
Subjects: LCSH: Greek Americans--New Mexico--Santa Fe--History--20th century.
Classification: LCC F805.G7 P66 2024 | DDC 978.9560089893--dc23/eng/20240605
LC record available at https://lccn.loc.gov/2024022262

WWW.SUNSTONEPRESS.COM
SUNSTONE PRESS / POST OFFICE BOX 2321 / SANTA FE, NM 87504-2321 /USA
(505) 988-4418

CONTENTS

PREFACE

AUTHOR'S PREFACE

Why did I write this book? And why 1914 to 1955?

I was born and raised in Santa Fe. My parents both came from Greece. My father was born in 1889 in the Village of Tragaki on the Greek island of Zakynthos, or Zante. He was a descendant of Venetian colonists who had settled there in 1510. My father Anastassios, or Tom, first came over to the United States in 1910, but went back to Greece in 1913 to fight for Greece in the Balkan Wars. He returned to the United States in 1914 and worked on the railroads and in the mines; but returned again to Europe in 1918, this time as an American soldier in the United States Expeditionary Forces. My father went back to Greece in 1929 to marry my mother Eleni, or Helen, and to bring her to America. They came to a foreign country thousands of miles from their homeland. They crossed the Mediterranean Sea and the massive Atlantic Ocean and landed on Ellis Island, New York City, on October 29, 1929! They then traveled three quarters across the United States to Denver. A year later, in 1930, they moved to Santa Fe, because, as they said, the Great Depression had not yet hit Santa Fe and the small town also reminded them of Greece. My father's brother Pete also came with them from Denver and the two brothers together opened a restaurant on the south side of the Plaza. They called it the Mayflower Café. In Chapter One I will relate the story of the Mayflower Café in detail. My parents had three children: Pete, James George, and Katherine. In 1934, their first child, Pete, died of Leukemia at the age of three. My father's brother Pete married Carmen, a non-Greek, and they had four children: Tom, Pete Jr., Barbara, and Diane. Their first child, Tom, died before his first birthday.

As a child, my playground was the Plaza, and I would often visit the New Mexico Museum of History in the Palace of the Governors. I remember looking at their dioramas of pre-historic Indian pueblos, and a mummified

Indian child who had been buried in a turkey feather blanket holding two ears of corn. Needless to say, this piqued my interest in archaeology. I also participated in the yearly celebration of the Fiesta (Fig. 1). This photo was taken during World War II. If you look closely, you can see two soldiers in the background. Also look closely at the two women sitting on a low wall. This wall surrounded the Plaza. The Plaza at that time was more than eighteen inches lower than it is today.

Figure 1.
The author dressed in Fiesta costume, c. 1945, on the Plaza in front of her father's Mayflower Café on the Plaza. Photo in author's collection.

I have lived on both coasts, California and Washington, DC and, after 20 years, returned to my home. On my return, I worked at the Maxwell Museum of Anthropology at the University of New Mexico, and when I retired, I began my own research projects. I received a Fellowship from the New Mexico State Historian's Office to research and write a book on the history of the Greeks of Albuquerque, which was published in 2012. More recently, I was asked by the Albuquerque Museum to curate an exhibit on a topic that both socially and economically impacted Albuquerque. Because tuberculosis (TB) and the railroad were the two leading forces impacting Albuquerque in the late nineteenth and early twentieth centuries, I chose the tuberculosis industry. There were seventeen TB sanatoriums in Albuquerque alone and fifty-four in New Mexico, and it was an industry! The exhibit opened in April 2017 and ran for six months.

Now, let's get back to why I wrote this book with my son Yorgos. My father and his brother opened the Mayflower Café on the south side of the Plaza in 1930 at 64 East San Francisco Street. In 1941 they moved next door to 66 East San Francisco Street. The latter address was previously the site of La Castrense, the Spanish military chapel built in 1760. The chapel had a beautiful altar screen, or reredos, carved by artisans who were brought from Mexico by Governor del Valle. The white stone for the reredos was quarried from the Jacona region of northern New Mexico, near Pojoaque. La Castrense was closed in 1835 and the reredos was moved down the street to the cathedral. In 1940 the reredos was again moved, this time to the newly built Cristo Rey Church on upper Canyon Road. If you haven't seen it, please do. I highly recommend it, especially since you know its history now. The Paso de Luz indoor mall, formerly the Arcade, now sits on the site where La Castrense was once located. There is a plaque on the outside wall of this building commemorating La Castrense.

I have a deep affection for Santa Fe and its fascinating history. I have seen many changes to the downtown area. You used to be able to go to the Plaza and do your grocery shopping. You could get your prescriptions filled at one of the three drug stores, which also had popular soda fountains—which were often filled with high school students as the current City Hall now occupies the buildings that were the original Santa Fe High School. There was a hardware store, a five-and-dime, fine clothing stores for men and women, a shoe store, and two or three cafes. If you needed to catch a train you could buy your ticket at the corner and the bus depot was just a block away on Water Street. There were a few curio shops and La Fonda for visitors, but mainly it was an old-fashioned downtown where locals came to meet and shop—and eat!

I knew the Greeks who were there in the 1930s, 40s, and 50s. Many were single men who have since disappeared without leaving families. Others left families, some of whom remained in Santa Fe and others who moved away. I became acutely aware of these circumstances when I wrote my previous book on the Greeks of Albuquerque. For that book I interviewed dozens of old timers, most of whom have since passed away. But at that time I realized there were few old timers left from Santa Fe to interview.

That saddened me. I had heard how they struggled, how they persevered, how they survived—or didn't—the ravages of the Great Depression, Tuberculosis (TB), and two world wars. Yet there was no one to tell their stories. I wanted people to know the history of the community I grew up in, the community that my parents helped build. My son Yorgos understood and helped me research and write this book.

Since these old timers were long gone, the only way to tell the story of these early Greeks was through historical sources. My son Yorgos helped me research these historical sources, and since I knew many of the old timers, I was able to ensure the completeness of the story. The information in this book came from three main historical sources: the *Santa Fe New Mexican* newspaper through newspaperarchive.com; Hudspeth's Santa Fe City Directories, and the U.S. Censuses, both through Ancestry.com. As I shall discuss in the Introduction, there were no Greeks in the 1900 and 1910 U.S. Censuses in Santa Fe, and there was one person, William Assimakis, from Greece in Santa Fe in the 1920 U.S. Census. My research later uncovered what appears to be one or two Greeks in Santa Fe around 1914, namely John Economou and Mr. Bachis (who may have been Italian) who purchased the Plaza Café and ran it until around 1915. But I was unable to find any more definite information about them. There is an Economou of a comparable age who later appears in California but I have no evidence that this was the same man who was in Santa Fe.

The Greeks didn't start showing up in numbers until the time of the 1930 U.S. Census. As I mentioned, my parents came to Santa Fe in 1930 and my father owned and operated the Mayflower Café on the Plaza from 1930 to 1952. After that, his partner at the time, Evangelos Klonis, owned and ran the cafe until 1955, after which the building was torn down.

By the 1940s, the number of Greeks coming to Santa Fe was exploding. There were also transients coming only for a year or two and then moving on. Partnerships were changing year-by-year, and I wonder how many times this was due to a game of Barbut, an overly-popular Greek dice game similar to Craps. Old timers were passing away. Keeping track of all of them becomes intractable by the 1950 Census.

I dedicate this book to the memories of the First Greeks of Santa Fe. Though

Santa Fe now has a Greek Orthodox Church (St. Elias the Prophet Greek Orthodox Church), there was no Greek Orthodox Church—an institution that still brings together Greek communities in the United States - in Santa Fe at that time. But the Santa Fe Greeks were a community. They celebrated at each others' homes. At Easter, the men would drive to Hyde Park and start roasting a lamb or a goat on a spit, and the women and children would arrive later for the picnic (Fig. 2). Together they celebrated Name Days (Saint's Days) and Holy days, where they would share food and play Greek music and dance, evoking feelings and memories of the Old Country from where they came.

Figure 2. Greeks from Albuquerque and Santa Fe, c. 1950 at Hyde Park. Photo in author's collection.

INTRODUCTION

INTRODUCTION

Why did the Greeks come to Santa Fe?

First, let's look at New Mexico to understand the context of Santa Fe. Why did the Greeks come to New Mexico? They came in at least two waves from 1880 to 1920. The first wave followed the railroad after it arrived in Albuquerque in 1880, to work in the mines and the lumber camps, or to service these new industries; and some came to attempt to recover from tuberculosis (TB). Greek miners included John Mastoras, John Torakis, Andrew Anitsakis, and Steve Pappas, all who worked at Colfax County mines; Mike Kartas, Antonio Andreakis, George Koklas, who worked at Walsenburg mines; and Tom, Pete, and Dan Pomonis who worked at Crosby, Wyoming mines. Some of these men had mined together and turned up together in Santa Fe years later, such as John Torakis and Andrew Anitsakis. The second wave often had relatives who had come with the first wave. Santa Fe Greeks eventually included numerous cousins from the Village of Kalloni on the Greek Island of Lesbos, namely Efterpi (Ethel) Kalangis, Nick Maryol, Theodore Peperas, Harry Dakos, and Gus Kalavantes—not to mention the Ipiotis brothers from Mytilene, Lesbos. Gus Razatos was related to the Razatos family in Denver, who had baptized my first brother when my parents were in Denver before they came to Santa Fe. Dan Razatos had an uncle in the same Razatos family in Denver, and Dan traveled to Santa Fe from Denver. John Hagidakis, Pete Dakis, and Antonio Andreakis were cousins. Tom and Pete Pomonis were brothers, not related to Dan Pomonis but the Pomonis name indicates origin from the Village of Tragaki on the Island of Zakynthos. According to the Encyclopedia of Zakynthos, the name Pomonis appeared in Tragaki in 1510, which corresponds to the time when Venice was sending colonists to occupy the Greek territory with Venetians.

But immigration from Greece was initially limited by U.S. law, so in the 1900 U.S. Census there was only one person from Greece living in New Mexico. That was Andrew Nelson, born in 1856, and working as a servant for the Vio family in Albuquerque on South First Street. He had come over only two years previously. With such an Anglo-Saxon name, you would think his parents were nineteenth-century British colonists from an Ionian Island—which was not at all as unlikely as it sounds. The British fleet defeated the French fleet in 1809 in a battle near the island of Zakynthos, and then went on to capture the Greek islands of Cephalonia, Kythira - and Zakynthos, which was its ancient pre-Greek name, or Zante as the Venetians called it when they occupied it in the centuries earlier. The next year the British captured the Greek island of Lefkada and, a few years later, Corfu. The 1815 Treaty between Great Britain and Russia gave Britain a protectorate over these Ionian Sea Islands and created a federation of the seven Ionian islands, known to Greeks as the Epta-Nissos (Seven-Islands): Corfu, Cephalonia, Kythira, Ithaca, Paxos, Lefkada, and Zakynthos.

By the time of the 1910 U.S. Census there were 167 people from Greece living in New Mexico. Almost all were found in Colfax County at Dawson or Van Houten or Koehler, working as miners. Only three were living elsewhere. Two men were miners in Mogollon, and a third, John Leras, was a confectioner in Silver City and he might have been New Mexico's first Greek businessman.

The 1920 U.S. Census found that there were 274 people from Greece living in New Mexico. By this time, more of them were restaurant workers or owners. Many of these men, such as Mike Keros and the Pomonis brothers, had learned these skills on the East Coast where they first disembarked or in a larger city such as Denver, before they relocated to New Mexico.

The 1930 U.S. Census found that there were 293 people from Greece living in New Mexico.

The 1940 U.S. Census found that there were 703 people from Greece living in New Mexico. Some of them would go on to serve with the U.S. Armed Forces in WWII.

The 1950 U.S. Census found that there were 414 people from Greece living in New Mexico. Immigration had peaked or slowed due to the war and the political situation in Greece. This was the beginning of the Cold War. Under the Truman Doctrine, the U.S. supported dictatorships in Greece, Turkey, and Iran, for the stated reason that it was necessary to keep these countries out of reach of the Soviet Union.

Greeks came to Santa Fe more slowly than they did to New Mexico. In the 1900 and 1910 U.S. Censuses, there were no people from Greece living in Santa Fe. In the 1920 U.S. Census, there was one person from Greece living in Santa Fe. That was William Arimakis (Assimakis), who was born in 1895, was brought over somewhere to the U.S. at age 4, and at age 25 in 1920 was then working as a laborer in a Santa Fe lumber camp. He did not appear in the 1930 Santa Fe Census but he did reappear with his wife Fanny in the 1940 Census.

According to the 1930 U.S. Census, there were 21 people from Greece living in Santa Fe (Table 1).

According to the 1940 Census, there were 58 people from Greece living in Santa Fe (Table 2).

According to the 1950 U.S. Census, there were 60 people from Greece living in Santa Fe (Table 3).

In the 1928-29 Santa Fe City Directory, there were 16 restaurants and three were owned by Greeks. In the 1930-31 Santa Fe City Directory, there were 18 restaurants and two were owned by Greeks. In the 1932-33 Santa Fe City Directory, there were 21 restaurants and four were owned by Greeks. In the 1934-35 Santa Fe City Directory there were 26 restaurants and nine were owned by Greeks. In the 1936-37 Santa Fe City Directory there were 25 restaurants and thirteen were owned by Greeks.

Name	Parent or spouse names	Birth Year	Relation to Head of House
Jim Karamanzio		approx. 1900	Lodger
John Giannario		approx. 1903	Guest
Nickolas D Carellas		approx. 1890	Head
Louis D Carellas		approx. 1888	Lodger
Steven Carman (Karman)		approx. 1900	Lodger
Harry Barsalis		approx. 1904	Lodger
John G Zervas		approx. 1887	Lodger
Gus G Razatos		approx. 1884	Lodger
Jim Ipiotis	Anastacia	approx. 1891	Head
Eva Caraman (Karman)		approx. 1904	Sister-in-law
Anastacia Ipiotis	Jim	approx. 1896	Wife
Constantine G Jumas		approx. 1906	Lodger
Lula Columbus	Pete	approx. 1892	Wife
Pete Columbus	Lula	approx. 1882	Head
Athan Meimary		approx. 1891	Lodger
Sam J Brown		approx. 1888	Lodger
Daniel Ronlous (?)		approx. 1907	Head
Konstantina Spelestopoulas		approx. 1897	Sister
John Legits	Mary	approx. 1890	Head
Earl Pongas		approx. 1890	Roomer
Guss L Pope	Verna	approx. 1888	Head

Table 1. According to the 1930 U.S. Census, there were 21 people from Greece living in Santa Fe. Many of these Greeks would go on to help build the businesses of downtown Santa Fe. My parents Tom and Helen Pomonis are not on this list. That year they moved from Denver to Santa Fe, but they were not on the Denver census either. Somehow the census missed them. My father's brother, Pete Pomonis, with whom my father owned and operated the Liberty Sandwich Shop in Denver, did appear in the Denver 1930 census.

Name	Parent or spouse names	Birth Year	Relation to Head of House
Nick E Morris	Eva	approx. 1890	Head
Dan Pomonis		approx. 1890	Lodger
Peter Pomonis	Carmen	approx. 1888	Head
Tom Pomonis	Helen	approx. 1890	Head
Helen Pomonis	Tom	approx. 1899	Wife
John Legits	Nellie	approx. 1890	Head
Dan Razatos	Phryne	approx. 1909	Head
Christos P Fettas	Medshu B	approx. 1895	Head
Sam A Anastas	Edna C	approx. 1899	Head
Geo Flongeris		approx. 1893	Lodger
Thomas Cruses		approx. 1901	Lodger
John Hagidakis		approx. 1896	Head
Nick Alexander		approx. 1898	Head
Mike Torakis		approx. 1887	Head
John Karvanos		approx. 1890	Head
Steve Goodas	Annie	approx. 1886	Head
Antonio Andreakis	Jeanette	approx. 1895	Head
Louis D Carellas	Edith	approx. 1891	Head
Gus Mitchell	Sally	approx. 1896	Head
William Assimakis	Fanny	approx. 1896	Head
Fanny Assimakis	William	approx. 1912	Wife
George Koklas		approx. 1890	Lodger
Steve Coukas	Mary	approx. 1889	Head
Earl Pongas	Vern	approx. 1892	Head
Mike Speratos	Ema	approx. 1891	Head
John Xurekes		approx. 1892	Head
Steven Korones	Candelaria	approx. 1892	Head
Pete B Anastas	Nona Mae	approx. 1895	Head
John Chavanos		approx. 1895	Head
Emmanuel Ntautis (Mike Dantis)		approx. 1895	Head
Sterie Koutroulis	Raynalda	approx. 1888	Head
Nick Galanos	Bernardita	approx. 1907	Head
James Ipiotis	Anastasia	approx. 1892	Head
Anastasia Ipiotis	James	approx. 1898	Wife
Saiomas (Spiros) Ipiotis		approx. 1895	Brother
Pete Colombus	Lula	approx. 1883	Head
Lula Colombus	Pete	approx. 1893	Wife
Paul Pagis		approx. 1890	Lodger
Alex Kalangis	Ethel	approx. 1899	Head
Ethel Kalangis	Alex	approx. 1912	Wife
Steve Anthony		approx. 1896	Lodger
Gust Kalavantis		approx. 1896	Lodger
Louis Zagaris		approx. 1891	Lodger
Antonios D Chegaras		approx. 1891	Lodger
Dennis Market	Evelyn	approx. 1896	Head
Pete C Dakis (Hadzidakis)		approx. 1933	
Mike Kartas	Alexandra	approx. 1884	Head
Alexandra Kartas	Mike	approx. 1897	Wife
Pete Theodore		approx. 1893	Head
Charles Hermes	Margaret	approx. 1895	Head
James Sitsas			
Pete Panaguton			
Tony Charnas or Chamas	Adie		
George Tsintsiras			
Thomas Bobas			
James Vosoras			
Isaak A Columbus	Louise F		

Table 2. According to the 1940 Census, there were 58 people from Greece living in Santa Fe.

Name	Relatives	Birth Year	Relation to Head of House
George Stamoulis	Betty	approx. 1913	Head
John Samaras		approx. 1897	
Tom Castriti		approx. 1901	
Alexandra Kartas	Esther	approx. 1898	Head
Nick Falaris		approx. 1901	
Jerome Travlos	Lucille, Joyce	approx. 1897	Head
Persephone Ganatos		approx. 1889	
Tom Monocrusos		approx. 1895	
C John Zervas		approx. 1885	
George M Christy	Lucille K	approx. 1883	Head
Nancy A Gianopoulos	Manuel	approx. 1928	
Harry Dakos	Vasso Z	approx. 1899	Head
Vasso Z Dakos	Harry	approx. 1926	Wife
Alex Kalangis	Ethel, Cornelia, Sarando	approx. 1901	Head
Ethel Kalangis	Alex, Cornelia, Sarando	approx. 1913	Wife
Lester Philips	Georgia, Sharon E	approx. 1914	Head
Louis Carellas	Edith	approx. 1890	Head
Gus T Mitchell	Sally T, Rosemary	approx. 1900	Head
George Chilimidos	Arretta E	approx. 1886	Head
Dennis Market	Evelyn	approx. 1897	Head
John Komis	Lemonia, Nick J	approx. 1915	Head
Lemonia Komis	John, Nick J	approx. 1923	Wife
Nick Chillemdas		approx. 1890	
Emanuel J Ntantis		approx. 1894	
Pete D Mavorpoulose	Georgia, Angelo	approx. 1893	Head
Georgia Mavropoulose	Pete D, Angelo	approx. 1893	Wife
George K Tsintsiras		approx. 1903	
Tomas A Langas		approx. 1899	
Antonio Andriakis	Janette		Head
Steve Anthony		approx. 1897	
Gus Volos		approx. 1891	
Louis Zagaris		approx. 1890	
Gus Palus		approx. 1900	
Gust Baltos		approx. 1905	
Gus Karos		approx. 1895	
James Brogolos		approx. 1909	
Jim Jargunes		approx. 1877	
Guss Thomas		approx. 1893	
Mike Torakis		approx. 1886	
Cleo Harris		approx. 1889	
Constantine Pavlou		approx. 1888	
Andy Dovas		approx. 1893	
George Virzoki		approx. 1887	
George K Kostolias		approx. 1894	
Andy P Anitsakis		approx. 1882	
Louis Paulos		approx. 1897	
Dan G Vorres		approx. 1896	
Mike Kaldo		approx. 1884	
Tom P Yanatos		approx. 1898	
Tom Pomonis	Helen, George, [Katherine]	approx. 1890	Head
Helen Pomonis	Tom, George, [Katherine]	approx. 1899	Wife
Angelo Klonis		approx. 1918	
Dan L Rozatos		approx. 1909	
Tony Mitchell	Bertha, Andrew	approx. 1895	Head
Steve Karonesa	Candelaria, Valentina	approx. 1890	Head
Earl Pongos	Verna May	approx. 1891	Head
Jerry Minetos	Precilla, Mary Helen	approx. 1908	Head
Nick Dantis	Beningna, Nick L	approx. 1891	Head
Steve Coukas	Lola or Mary	approx. 1892	Head

Table 3. According to the 1950 U.S. Census, there were 60 people from Greece living in Santa Fe.

SAN FRANCISCO

1

A Walk Down East San Francisco Street, Along the Plaza from Old Santa Fe Trail (aka Shelby Street) to Lincoln Avenue

I begin this first chapter with this short Preamble, a preamble to an amble down "History Lane at the End of the Santa Fe Trail."

Many would be surprised to learn that Greek immigrants contributed significantly to the multi-cultural post-European contact era of Santa Fe, and specifically, to the development of twentieth-century Santa Fe. There were at least forty-eight Greek immigrant-owned businesses in the 1910s through the 1950s in and around downtown Santa Fe.

This book is a walking tour of those Greek immigrant-owned businesses in downtown Santa Fe from the 1910s through the 1950s (Map 1). Most of the addresses are still in use, but the businesses occupying them certainly have changed. I will be emphasizing businesses that were Greek-owned but I will mention other selected businesses to provide you with context.

If you have only an hour or two, I recommend walking along the Plaza on East San Francisco Street (Chapter 1) and Lincoln Avenue (Chapter 2). You will also enjoy reading the two short chapters on the history of the Plaza (Chapters 3 and 4).

If you have additional time, you can continue walking down West San Francisco Street (Chapter 5), and then make your way down Galisteo Street (Chapter 6), Water Street (Chapter 7), and Don Gaspar Avenue (Chapter 8).

If you are interested in a continuation of this history, then you can follow the tour to Agua Fria (Chapter 9) and Cerrillos Road (Chapter 10).

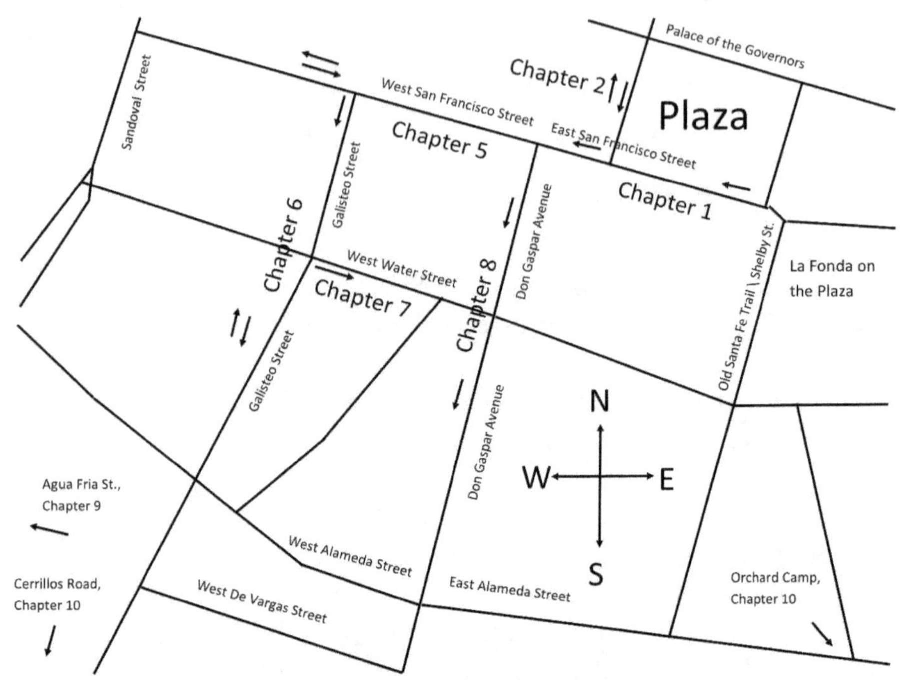

Map 1. The complete walking tour.

Old Santa Fe Trail/Shelby Street at East San Francisco Street.

We begin our walking tour by starting at the southeast corner of the Plaza at La Fonda Hotel (Map 2, Fig. 3). We cross the Old Santa Fe Trail (which used to be called Shelby Street) toward the Plaza, and follow East San Francisco Street westward. The Plaza is on our right, The Cathedral Basilica of Saint Francis of Assisi and La Fonda are behind us to the east, as are the Santa Fe mountains. Tip: you can install a compass app on your smartphone.

The first business we come to, on the corner, is 84 East San Francisco Street. In 1915, it was occupied by a small department store called Seligman Bros. (Fig. 4). The address was later occupied by Blatt Beauty Shop in 1930, then Strombergs in 1940 and then Leed's Shoe Store in 1947.

Next door is 82 East San Francisco Street. Note that the addresses are decreasing because we are walking toward the end of East San Francisco Street and the beginning of West San Francisco Street.

In the 1910s to 1950s, 82 East San Francisco Street was occupied by the Capital Pharmacy (Fig. 5) with its famous soda fountain. Depending on the time of day, the pharmacy's soda counter was full of high school students, as Santa Fe High School was located two blocks north in what is now City Hall!

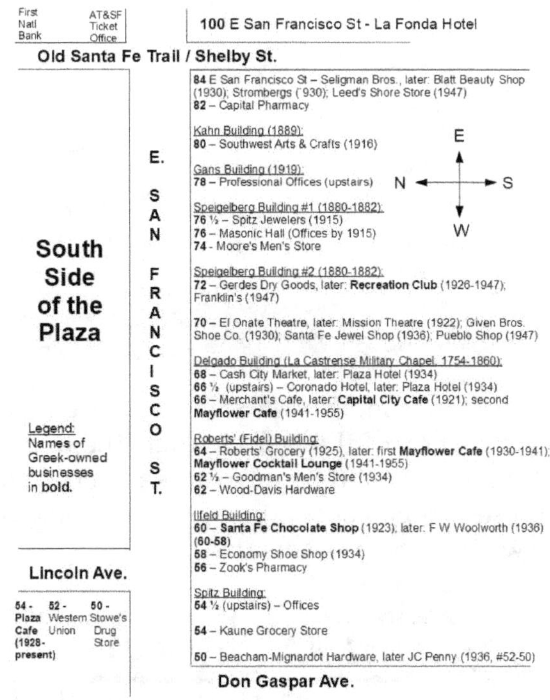

Map 2. East San Francisco Street.
Building names, when there are any, are underlined.

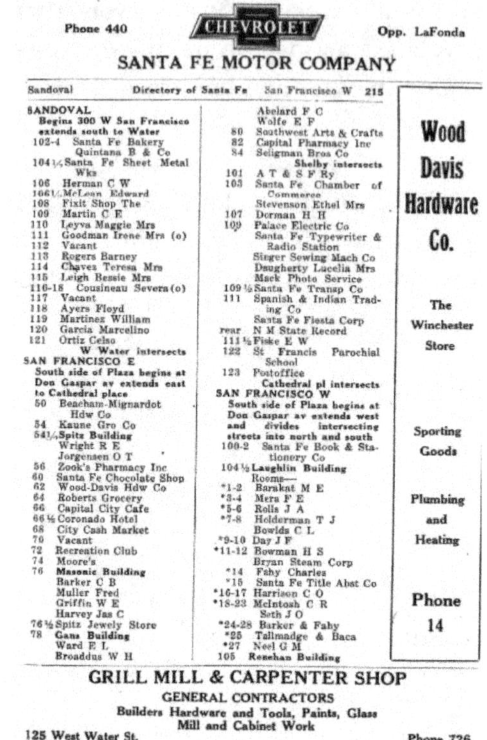

Phone 440 CHEVROLET Opp. LaFonda

SANTA FE MOTOR COMPANY

Sandoval Directory of Santa Fe San Francisco W 215

SANDOVAL
Begins 300 W San Francisco extends south to Water
102-4 Santa Fe Bakery
Quintana B & Co
104½ Santa Fe Sheet Metal Wks
106 Herman C W
106½ McLean Edward
108 Fixit Shop The
109 Martin C E
110 Leyva Maggie Mrs
111 Goodman Irene Mrs (o)
112 Vacant
113 Rogers Barney
114 Chaves Teresa Mrs
115 Leigh Bessie Mrs
116-18 Cousineau Severa (o)
117 Vacant
118 Ayers Floyd
119 Martinez William
120 Garcia Marcelino
121 Ortiz Celso
W Water intersects

SAN FRANCISCO E
South side of Plaza begins at Don Gaspar av extends east to Cathedral place
50 Beacham-Mignardot Hdw Co
54 Kaune Gro Co
54½ **Spitz Building**
Wright R E
Jorgensen O T
56 Zook's Pharmacy Inc
60 Santa Fe Chocolate Shop
62 Wood-Davis Hdw Co
64 Roberts Grocery
66 Capital City Cafe
66½ Coronado Hotel
68 City Cash Market
70 Vacant
72 Recreation Club
74 Moore's
76 **Masonic Building**
Barker C B
Muller Fred
Griffin W E
Harvey Jas C
76½ Spitz Jewely Store
78 **Gans Building**
Ward E L
Broaddus W H
Abelard F C
Wolfe E F
80 Southwest Arts & Crafts
82 Capital Pharmacy Inc
84 Seligman Bros Co
Shelby intersects
101 A T & S F Ry
103 Santa Fe Chamber of Commerce
Stevenson Ethel Mrs
107 Dorman H H
109 Palace Electric Co
Santa Fe Typewriter & Radio Station
Singer Sewing Mach Co
Daugherty Lucelia Mrs
Mack Photo Service
109½ Santa Fe Transp Co
111 Spanish & Indian Trading Co
Santa Fe Fiesta Corp
rear N M State Record
111½ Fiske E W
122 St Francis Parochial School
123 Postoffice
Cathedral pl intersects

SAN FRANCISCO W
South side of Plaza begins at Don Gaspar av extends west and divides intersecting streets into north and south
100-2 Santa Fe Book & Stationery Co
104½ **Laughlin Building**
Rooms—
*1-2 Barakat M E
*3-4 Mera F E
*5-6 Rolls J A
*7-8 Holderman T J
Bowlds C L
*9-10 Day J F
*11-12 Bowman H S
Bryan Steam Corp
*14 Fahy Charles
*15 Santa Fe Title Abst Co
*16-17 Harrison C O
*18-23 McIntosh C R
Seth J O
*24-28 Barker & Fahy
*25 Tallmadge & Baca
*27 Neel G M
105 **Renehan Building**

Wood Davis Hardware Co.
The Winchester Store
Sporting Goods
Plumbing and Heating
Phone 14

GRILL MILL & CARPENTER SHOP
GENERAL CONTRACTORS
Builders Hardware and Tools, Paints, Glass
Mill and Cabinet Work
125 West Water St. Phone 726

Figure 3. Page from Hudspeth's 1928 Santa Fe City Directory, showing the addresses of this portion of the walking tour. The tour begins at 84 East San Francisco Street (Seligman Bros Co) at the intersection with Old Santa Fe Trail, which used to be called Shelby Street. Look in the upper right column for the words "Shelby intersects."

Figure 4. Advertisement for Seligman Bros Co. *Santa Fe New Mexican*, August 7, 1915.

Figure 5. Advertisement for Capital Pharmacy. *Santa Fe New Mexican*, Jan. 3, 1927.

The Kahn Building

We now walk past the Kahn Building. This building was erected in the Italianate style in 1889 and remodeled around 1930 in the Spanish Colonial style.

The first tenants of this new building in 1890 were: Kahn himself on the west; Spitz Jewelry, which had moved from another site and would move again into the Seligman Building next door; the Masonic Hall on the second floor which would also move; and a saloon put in by E. Henolt of New Orleans. But by 1916 they had all moved out.

From 1916 through the 1950s, 80 East San Francisco Street was the site of Southwest Arts & Crafts (Fig. 6). It was established in 1916 by trader Julius Gans. It was very popular because of the Native American artisans demonstrating in the shop. From the ground floor, you could watch Native Americans weaving below in a central recess.

Figure 6. Advertisement for Southwest Arts & Crafts. *Santa Fe New Mexican*, Dec. 30, 1921.

Gans Building and Spiegelberg Buildings #1 and #2

We now come to 78 East San Francisco Street and the Gans building. This "building" is a second floor addition to the first Spiegelberg Building (#1). Built in 1919 by Julius Gans of Southwest Arts & Crafts, it housed professional offices.

72-76 East San Francisco Street and the two Spiegelberg buildings were built from 1880 to 1882. Originally Italianate in style, John Gaw Meem modified them with facades: 74-76 East San Francisco Street in 1952 in the Territorial style; and 72 East San Francisco Street in 1960 in the Spanish Colonial style. The first Spiegelberg Building (#1) at 74-76 East San Francisco Street was later referred to as the Masonic Building. These two Spiegelberg buildings housed Spitz Jewelry at 76 ½, a Masonic Temple (Hall) at 76, Moore's the Men's Store at 74, and, at 72, "the old Gerdes Store landmark" (Gerdes Dry Goods Co.), which was replaced by the Recreation Club in 1926 and later, starting in 1947, Franklin's, a women's clothing store. The Masonic Hall functioned from 1890 (Fig. 7) to at least 1915 when the building was remodeled (Fig. 8). This portion of East San Francisco Street was referred to as the Kahn block in 1895. It housed numerous businesses over the years (Figs. 9, 10).

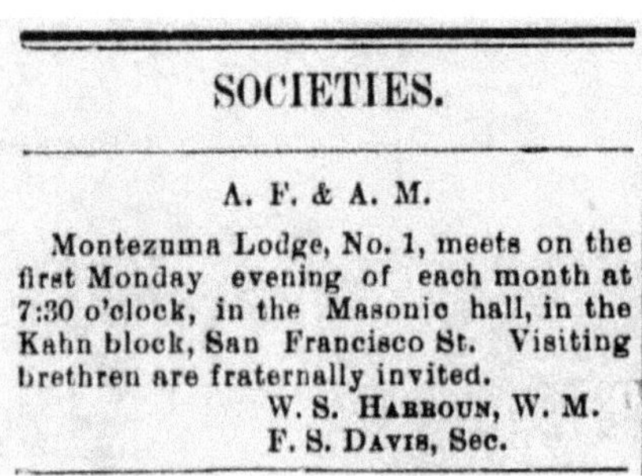

SOCIETIES.

A. F. & A. M.

Montezuma Lodge, No. 1, meets on the first Monday evening of each month at 7:30 o'clock, in the Masonic hall, in the Kahn block, San Francisco St. Visiting brethren are fraternally invited.

W. S. Harroun, W. M.
F. S. Davis, Sec.

Figure 7.
Advertisement for a meeting of Montezuma Lodge.
Santa Fe New Mexican, April 12, 1890.

MASONIC BUILDING
ENTIRELY REMODELED

The "Blue Lodge" Masonic Temple on San Francisco street is being remodeled under direction of Contractor August Reingardt at a cost of $11,000. The fronts will be taken out and placed in the rear and handsome modern store fronts installed; new floors, ceiling, painting, wiring and plumbing are included and the Santa Fe Hardware & Supply company will install a new heating plant. Hardwood floors will be placed in the lodge rooms and the building practically made new. It is understood Mr. Spitz will likely occupy one of the store rooms when completed.

Figure 8. Notice for the Masonic Building. *Santa Fe New Mexican*, 1915.

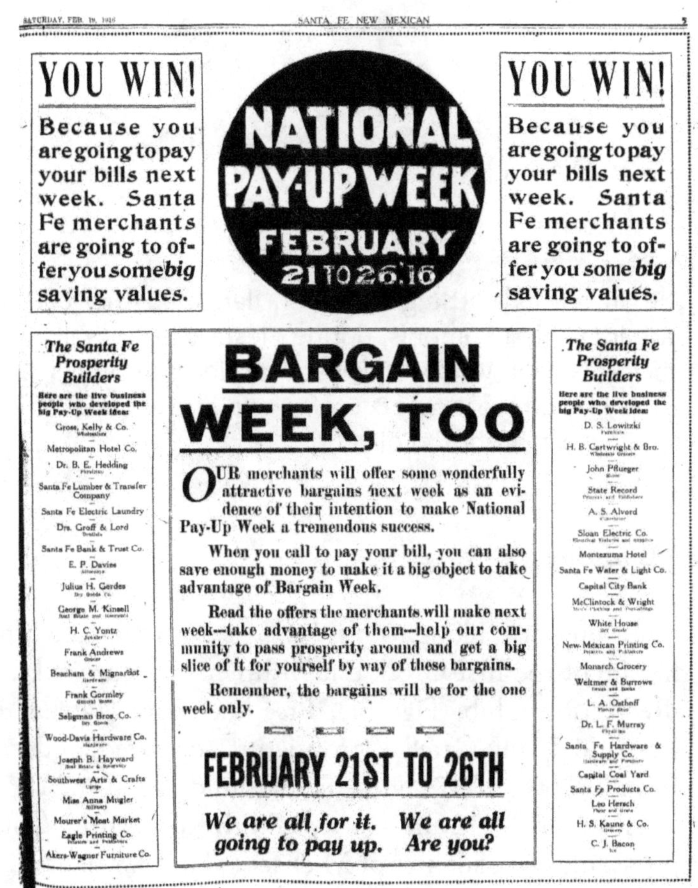

Figure 9.
Advertisement for downtown businesses.
Santa Fe New Mexican, Feb. 12, 1916.

Figure 10. The author as a little girl, center, flanked by her cousins Diane (left) and Barbara (right) Pomonis, during Fiesta c. 1945 walking west on East San Francisco Street. Visible business signs include Leed's Shoe Store, Capital Pharmacy, Southwest Arts & Crafts, and professional offices in the Gans building. Photo in author's collection.

Spiegelberg Building #2

The next address on our walking tour is 72 East San Francisco Street. This address is the site of the first Greek establishment on our walk along the Plaza. The Recreation Club (Fig. 11), first known as Carellas Brothers Billiards, Nick and Louis Carellas proprietors, operated under Carellas ownership from 1926 to 1947. Nick died around age 40 in 1931. Louis divorced his first wife in 1932 and married Edith Koklas from Colorado in 1932 or 1933. Edith was daughter of Michael (Matthew) S. and Christine (Dolly) M. Koklas. Willy Rounseville married Edith's sister Victoria in 1936, making Rounseville and Carellas brothers-in-law. Willy Rounseville then joined Louis Carellas as a partner in the Recreation Club. Michael

Koklas' brother, George Koklas, who moved to Santa Fe in 1933 and who died there in 1959, also joined as a partner. George never married.

The Koklases had lived in Oakview, Colorado in 1920 and then La Veta, Colorado in 1930, where Michael had been a miner and then a truck driver. Between 1940 and 1942, Michael and Christine Koklas moved to Santa Fe. Michael, Louis Carellas' father-in-law, then joined the Recreation Club as a partner. Michael's wife Christine was born in Italy or France in 1892, and immigrated in 1910.

In 1946 the Recreation Club moved to 221 Galisteo Street.

According to Rounseville, the Recreation Club wasn't just a pool hall. People—businessmen, politicians including Governors of the State—would go there to socialize, check baseball scores that were coming in on a ticker tape, or buy chewing tobacco. They also came in to gamble. According to the *Santa Fe New Mexican*, on June 14, 1940, the Santa Fe City Police raided the Recreation Club, along with the Lensic Tavern and the Mission Pool Hall, where they arrested twenty-seven patrons for illegal gambling. At the Recreation Club, police confiscated Blackjack, Craps, and Barbut tables; $350 in players' moneys; and arrested fifteen players and three operators. Previously that week, police had already raided the three establishments and confiscated four slot machines.

The Greeks, including my father, and others, would sometimes gamble in a back room of the Mayflower Café late into the night. If Papa won, he would come home and place a stack of money under my mother's pillow.

In 1938, Louis Zagaris was listed as a clerk at the Recreation Club. In 1947, he became a partner with Antonio Andreakis in the Yucca Bar on Galisteo Street and was still working in 1957. He was born in 1890 passed in 1969.

From 1932 to 1936, Paul G. Pagis (Pages) was a clerk at the Recreation Club. In 1938, and 1942 through 1944, he was a waiter at the Mayflower Café. In between, in 1940, he was an owner of the Lensic Sandwich Shop. In 1947 he was a waiter at the Recreation Club. He was born in 1885 in Sparta, Greece and passed in 1947.

Figure 11. Advertisement for the Recreation Club.
Santa Fe New Mexican, Sept. 26, 1938.

The Delgado Building

We now come to 70-66 East San Francisco Street and the Delgado Building. We begin with a brief discussion of the history of the site.

This address was the site of La Castrense military chapel from 1754 to 1860. The chapel was called La Castrense Nuestra Señora de la Luz or Most Holy Mother of Light. See if you can find the historic plaque that marks the location. The chapel had a beautiful altar screen or reredos carved by artisans, including Spanish Agent Jose Mierra y Pacheco. These artisans were brought from Mexico by Governor Marin del Valle. The white stone of the altar screen is volcanic rock or "pumice" from the Valles Caldera eruptions. It was quarried from the Jaconita region near Pojoaque on the road to Los Alamos.

La Castrense was closed by 1835 because the Mexican government withdrew its support for churches and clergy in New Mexico, resulting in deterioration of the chapel's structure through neglect. The most serious problem of New Mexico during the Mexican period that followed the Spanish period was the lack of adequate finances from the Mexican government to maintain the bare essentials of the New Mexican government. The Mexican government withdrew support for the clergy, many who came from Spain, because the government suspected the clergy would continue to be loyal to the Spanish Crown.

By the late 1850s, La Castrense was used by U.S. forces as an ammunition storeroom and then as a district court. By 1859, the stone reredos was removed and placed in the sanctuary of La Parroquia, the church which was replaced by St. Francis Cathedral. In 1940, this reredos was moved into Cristo Rey Church at the top of Canyon Road, which had been designed specifically to house the reredos. Cristo Rey Church is the largest modern adobe structure designed by John Gaw Meem. It took 180,000 adobes to build, with most of the work done by the people of that area.

The chapel La Castrense on the Plaza was deconsecrated and the building sold to don Simón Delgado in 1860. A photo from c. 1866 shows the adobe side walls and high windows of the old chapel (Palace of the Governors Photo Archives, NMHM/DCA, Negative No. 038178.).

Remember, we are at the Delgado Building, 70-66 East San Francisco Street.

70 East San Francisco Street in the 1910s and early 1920s was the site of the El Onate Theatre. That theatre closed and reopened on May 1, 1922 as the Mission Theatre (Fig. 12). The Mission operated through 1927. In 1928, the space was vacant. In 1930, it was occupied by the Given Bros. Shoe Co. In 1934, the space was vacant (Imagine space on the Plaza being vacant today!). In 1936, it was occupied by the Santa Fe Jewel Shop, which went out of business in 1944, and then it was occupied by 1947 by the Pueblo Shop.

Figure 12.
Advertisement for the Mission Theatre.
Santa Fe New Mexican, January 3, 1927.

The next set of addresses on our walk along the Plaza is 68-66 East San Francisco Street. Prior to 1934, 66 East San Francisco Street housed the Coronado Hotel, after which it was owned and operated by Louis Richard as the Plaza Hotel and the address was changed to 66 ½. The lobby of the hotel was downstairs and the rooms were upstairs. Some Greek roomers, such as Theofani (Thee) Keris (Keros), Pete Theodore of the Mayflower Café and Cocktail Lounge next door, Gust Razatos, and John Komis, were long-time residents. In the 1930 U.S. Census, there were 20 people staying at the Plaza Hotel, six of whom were Greek (Table 4). We cover all six men in this book except for Harry Barsalis, who appeared only in this 1930 census entry. He was listed as working as a waiter at an unnamed business.

Household Members (Name)	Age	Relationship
Loris Richard	35	Head
John G Zervas *	43	Lodger
Harry B Cook	55	Lodger
Harry Barsalis *	26	Lodger
Steven Carman *	30	Lodger
Lindsey K Newton	25	Lodger
Jose Cabrieres	19	Lodger
Moises Rodriguez	21	Lodger
Fred Galvez	28	Lodger
John Giannario *	27	Guest
Gus G Rozates *	46	Lodger
H W Clark	31	Lodger
Jim Karamanzio *	30	Lodger
Lucy Sena	39	Sister
Ida I Grosshans	62	Mother
John B Grosshans	21	Son
Adolf Torres	26	Lodger
John C Scott	75	Lodger
Bernarda Griego	21	Lodger
Jose Lino Romero	44	Lodger
Loris Richard	35	Head
John G Zervas *	43	Lodger
Harry B Cook	55	Lodger
Harry Barsalis *	26	Lodger
Steven Carman *	30	Lodger
Lindsey K Newton	25	Lodger
Jose Cabrieres	19	Lodger
Moises Rodriguez	21	Lodger
Fred Galvez	28	Lodger
John Giannario *	27	Guest
Gus G Rozates *	46	Lodger
H W Clark	31	Lodger
Jim Karamanzio *	30	Lodger
Lucy Sena	39	Sister
Ida I Grosshans	62	Mother
John B Grosshans	21	Son
Adolf Torres	26	Lodger
John C Scott	75	Lodger
Bernarda Griego	21	Lodger
Jose Lino Romero	44	Lodger

Table 4. 1930 U.S. Census entries for the Plaza Hotel. Greeks are marked with an asterisk (*).

Thee Karis told us that the men would stay up late gambling in one of the hotel rooms, and would order in sandwiches from the Plaza Café.

66 East San Francisco Street was occupied prior to August 1921 by a non-Greek business, the Merchants Café. In August 1921, the restaurant at this address was reopened as the Capital City Café, by Alex Janos, Nicholas Triantis, and John Kouteles. Sometime in 1922, ownership changed to the Greek restaurateur John Legits (Leggitt). In late 1926, Legits temporarily closed the cafe for "extensive repairs," reopening in early 1927 resulting in "the most up-to-date cafe in Santa Fe with complete new equipment from front to back." (Fig. 13) Legits ran the Capital City Café to 1940 (Fig. 14).

Legits was born in 1889 and moved to the United States from Greece at age 16. In 1918, at age 29 he contracted tuberculosis and moved from Charleston, West Virgina to Albuquerque, to stay at a sanatorium. In 1922 he moved to Santa Fe and bought the Capital City Café. At age 37 he married Nellie Sena with whom he had six children. Legits died in 1941 at age 52 after a long illness.

George Pappas was a chef for the Capital City Café in 1936.

Constantine "Gus" Jumas was a cook for the café from about 1930 through at least 1934. He was born in 1906 in Greece, immigrated in 1921, and had his first papers in 1930.

Re-Opening

CAPITAL CITY CAFE

announces

THEIR RE-OPENING

AT 5:30 P. M. TODAY

After Having Been Closed the Past Several Weeks
Undergoing Extensive Re-modeling

Figure 13. Advertisement for the Capital City Café. *Santa Fe New Mexican*, Jan. 15, 1927.

Figure 14. Advertisement for the Capital City Café. *Santa Fe New Mexican*, March 14, 1936.

From 1928 to 1933, Legits took Pete Columbus (wife Toula) as partner in the Capital City Café. Born in 1882, Columbus later went on to open the Candyland on Lincoln Avenue.

From 1928 to 1929, Legits also took Guss Pope (wife Verna) as partner. Pope was born around 1887 in Greece and immigrated in 1905. In 1920 Pope was in Yellowstone, Montana, working as a waiter and married to Verna Pope (nee Mae Bruner) whom he had married around 1917. An article appears in the Las Vegas Daily Optic, March 26, 1929, stated that Konstantine Andrew Papdimitru became a U.S. citizen and changed the eleven letter Konstantine to the three letter Gus, and changed the eleven letter Papdimitriu to the four letter Pope.

Living with Guss Pope and his wife Verna in 1928 and 1930 at 215 West Manhattan as a roomer was Earl Pongas. Pongas was born in 1891 in Greece and came to the U.S. in 1907. He ran the New York Confectionary with Paul Calas in 1916 in Paris, Texas. He served for the U.S. in WW I, after which he moved to Webb City, Missouri, and worked at the Minerva Candy Company. In 1921, Pongas had a kidney operation in Des Moines, Iowa, and was admitted to a government TB sanatorium. By 1928, Pongas had moved to Santa Fe and was a roomer with Guss and Verna Pope. In 1933, Verna filed for divorce against Gus, and in the 1934 Santa Fe City Directory, Earl and Verna Pongas are living at 332 Delgado. In 1971, in Earl's obituary, he is said to be survived by his wife Verna. As it turns out, Pope was Verna's second husband and her second divorce, and Pongas was her third husband. Verna apparently had a sweet tooth for Greek confectioners and her third marriage to Pongas was a long and happy one.

Roberts Building

The next building on our walking tour, the Roberts Building at 64-62 East San Francisco Street, was owned by Louis Roberts. Roberts bought the building in July 1925 from the Fidel brothers, owners of the El Fidel Hotel on Galisteo Street.

64 East San Francisco Street was occupied from 1925 to 1928 by Roberts Grocery (Fig. 15), Louis Roberts, proprietor. The grocery had been operating since 1922 but probably in a different location. Roberts bought the building on Plaza and moved his grocery store there in July 1925. Roberts was an African-American who later ran a car lot.

In 1930, Roberts vacated 64 East San Francisco Street and rented it out to Tom and Pete Pomonis. It was there that Tom and Pete opened the first Mayflower Café. Ten years later, in 1940, the Capital City Café next door at 66 East San Francisco Street closed. The Pomonis brothers then closed their first Mayflower Café and reopened it at 66 East San Francisco Street. They also opened the Mayflower Cocktail Lounge at their old location at 64 East San Francisco Street. (Figs. 16-24).

ROBERTS' GROCERY

Bakery, Market and Delicatessen

WE DELIVER

Grocery Phones, 3 and 4 **Market Phone 740**

Extra Special Prices for Saturday on Fancy Cookies—ask the clerks about them.

Bananas, 3 lbs. for **25c**
Plums, 2 lbs. for **25c**
Peaches, 2 lbs. for **25c**
Grapes, per lb. **15c**
Green Apples, 3 lbs for **25c**
Large Cantaloupes, 2 for **25c**
Fresh Tomatoes, per lb **15c**
Bunch Carrots, Turnips, Beets, per bunch .... **.5c**
Fresh Peas, per lb **10c**
Fresh Green Beans, 2 lbs. for **25c**
Fresh Spinach, 2 lbs. for **25c**

Our Bakery line is complete. The best of breads, fancy cakes, rolls, cookies, pies, doughnuts, etc.

MEAT DEPARTMENT

Fresh Hamburger, per lb **15c**
Chuck Roast, per lb. **20c**
Beef Boil, per lb **15c**
Short Ribs, per lb. **10c**
Lamb Hearts, per lb. **15c**
Bacon Squares, per lb **20c**
Swift's Hams, per lb **28c**
Swift's Bacon, per lb **32c**
Longhorn Cheese, per lb **35c**

Hens, Broilers, Fryers, Belgian Hares
WE DELIVER

J. R. ROBERTS

SOUTH SIDE PLAZA

Figure 15. Advertisement for Robert's Grocery Store.
Santa Fe New Mexican, July 13, 1928.

Figure 16. Advertisement for the reopening of the Mayflower Café. *Santa Fe New Mexican*, May 4, 1940.

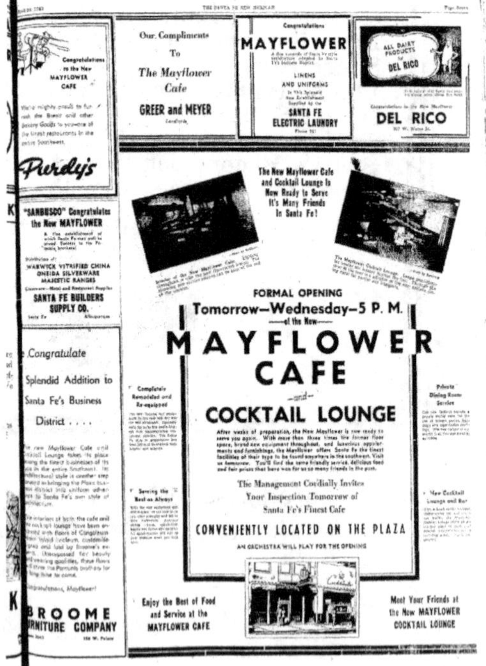

Congratulations to the New MAYFLOWER CAFE

Purdy's

Our Compliments To The Mayflower Cafe

GREER and MEYER

Landlords

Congratulations

MAYFLOWER

LINENS AND UNIFORMS

SANTA FE ELECTRIC LAUNDRY

ALL DAIRY PRODUCTS by DEL RICO

DEL RICO

"SANBUSCO" Congratulates the New MAYFLOWER

WARWICK VITRIFIED CHINA
ONEIDA SILVERWARE
MAJESTIC RANGES

SANTA FE BUILDERS SUPPLY CO.

Santa Fe — Albuquerque

The New Mayflower Cafe and Cocktail Lounge Is Now Ready to Serve It's Many Friends In Santa Fe!

Congratulate

Splendid Addition to Santa Fe's Business District . . . .

Congratulations, Mayflower!

BROOME FURNITURE COMPANY

Completely Remodeled and Re-equipped

Serving the Best as Always

FORMAL OPENING

Tomorrow—Wednesday—5 P. M.

—of the New—

MAYFLOWER CAFE

—and—

COCKTAIL LOUNGE

After weeks of preparation, the New Mayflower is now ready to serve you again. With more than three times the former floor space, brand new equipment throughout, and luxurious appointments and furnishings, the Mayflower offers Santa Fe the finest facilities of their type to be found anywhere in the southwest. Visit us tomorrow. You'll find the same friendly service, delicious food and fair prices that have won for us so many friends in the past.

The Management Cordially Invites Your Inspection Tomorrow of Santa Fe's Finest Cafe

CONVENIENTLY LOCATED ON THE PLAZA

AN ORCHESTRA WILL PLAY FOR THE OPENING

Private Dining Room Service

New Cocktail Lounge and Bar

Enjoy the Best of Food and Service at the MAYFLOWER CAFE

Meet Your Friends at the New MAYFLOWER COCKTAIL LOUNGE

Figure 17. Advertisement for the Mayflower Café. *Santa Fe New Mexican*, April 30, 1940.

Figure 18. 1940 reopening of the Mayflower Café. The entrance to the Cocktail Lounge is at the far right. From right to left: Pete Theodore, unknown woman, Tom Pomonis, Carmen Pomonis, Pete Pomonis (black suit). Photo in author's collection.

Figure 19. 1940 reopening of the Mayflower Café. Photo in author's

Figure 20.
Interior of the Mayflower Cocktail Lounge, c. 1940.
Photo in author's collection.

Figure 21.
Interior of the Mayflower Cocktail Lounge, c. 1940.
Photo in author's collection.

Figure 22. Interior of the Mayflower Cocktail Lounge, c. 1940. From left to right: Esther Kartas, Mike Kartas, Alexandra Kartas, Mike Falaris, unknown, Andy Ganatos, Pete Theodore. Photo in author's collection.

CHRISTMAS

GREETINGS

...The best for you and yours is the sincere wish of every member of this firm. Our Christmas present has already been received...your fine patronage all year and during the Holiday Season has made us happy at Christmas time. So, please accept our thanks along with this Greeting.

AND BEST WISHES FOR

A Happy New Year

Mr. and Mrs. Pete S. Pomonis	Dan Pomonis
Mr. and Mrs. Tom Pomonis	Henry Mares
Mr. and Mrs. Pete Theodore	Pete Brown
AND THE STAFF:	Joe Tapia
Lucille Roberts	Andrew Ganetos
Dorothy Kimbrough	John W. Jordan
Sara Brannon	William Alafais
Eva Cahill	James Filias
Laura Synder	Phillip Pomonis
Bessie Collamer	George Markis
Hazel Baca	Perfecto Martinez
Angel Alice	Frank Gonzales
Jessie Baca	Tom Yanatos
Marie Stephens	Macario Velarde
Irene Henson	Benny Martinez
Spiro Felopoulos	Ascencion Vigil

THE

MAYFLOWER

CAFE AND COCKTAIL LOUNGE

BAR OPEN ALL DAY CHRISTMAS DAY

Figure 23. Christmas greeting from the staff of the Mayflower Café. December 24, 1940, *Santa Fe New Mexican*.

THIS IS TO GIVE THANKS

Thanks For Our Freedom Thanks For The Blessings We All Enjoy Thanks For The American Way Of Life.

* * *

WE GIVE THANKS TO OUR FRIENDS FOR THEIR PATRONAGE, AND FOR THE NEW FRIENDS THEY BROUGHT US DURING THE YEAR

Carmen Pomonis
Pete Theodore

And Thanks from our staff—to their customers.
Angel Allen - Rose Wininger - George Peros - Louie Frangos

* * *

WHEN THE CHILL WINDS HURL YOU ALONG SAN FRANCISCO STREET, STOP IN FOR A HOT DRINK AT

SANTA FE'S NEWEST & BEST
Mayflower
Cocktail Lounge

Hot Buttered Rum
Hot Toddies
And Other
Hot Drinks

Complete Stock of
Packaged Goods,
Domestic & Imported

Figure 24.
Advertisement for the Mayflower Café.
Santa Fe New Mexican, Nov. 26, 1947.

Tom worked in the mines in Crosby, Wyoming after returning in 1918 from France, where he fought as an American soldier in the American Expeditionary Forces in WWI. By 1924, according to the Denver City Directory, Tom was a baker and Pete was a clerk in Denver. Pete married Pearl in 1924. In 1927, the two brothers appeared as proprietors, along with Pete Yulatos, of Pomonis & Yulatos, which is variously listed in the Denver City Directory as a confectionary and as a restaurant. The business was short-lived, because by 1928 the Pomonis brothers were now running the Liberty Sandwich Shop, which in 1930 was listed as the Liberty Sandwich & Candy Shop. In 1929, Tom returned to the Greek island on which he was born, Zakynthos, to marry Helen Vorres, and they returned to Denver but did not appear in the 1930 Denver City Directory. There in Denver they had their first child, Pete, who later passed at age 3 in Santa Fe from Leukemia. Pete and Pearl Pomonis divorced in December 1930. Also in the latter part of 1930, the Pomonis brothers along with Tom's new wife Helen moved to Santa Fe, where as previously stated, they opened the Mayflower Café on the Plaza. They had heard that the Great Depression had not yet hit Santa Fe, and when they arrived, the small town reminded them of Greece.

During WWII, the Mayflower Café had a contract with the U.S. Army to serve meals to Selective Service inductees who were receiving physical examinations at Bruns General Hospital in Santa Fe before shipping out to basic training. I remember the big trucks coming and parking in front of the café. The boys would pile out of the back of the trucks and through the front door into the back of the café where the banquet room was set aside for them. That contract meant a lot to my father, not just for business reasons, but also for the fact that he was a veteran of the Balkan Wars in which he fought for Greece; and my father Tom also enlisted with the U.S. Army and served with the American Expeditionary Forces in France as an ambulance driver. He was proud to know that he would be buried at the U.S. National Cemetery in Santa Fe. Like many Greek immigrants, he supported the war effort in many ways, such as by buying war bonds, and participating in auctions to benefit the troops. He was reported to have offered to give $125 to the first five New Mexico soldiers to land in Greece during WWII. Bruns General Hospital (Figs. 25, 26), or Bruns Army Hospital, was opened in April 1943 to treat soldiers arriving from the WWII

Pacific Theatre, such as the 200th Coast Artillery Battalion survivors of the Bataan Death March. The hospital was named after Army physician Col. Earl Harvey Bruns, who was an expert on pulmonary tuberculosis and who died from the disease a decade earlier. Bruns General Hospital had been an economic powerhouse in New Mexico. Employing 600 military men and 1000 civilians and boasting 2500 beds, it brought $4.5 million annually into the New Mexico economy. Despite public protest, the hospital was decommissioned shortly after the end of the war.

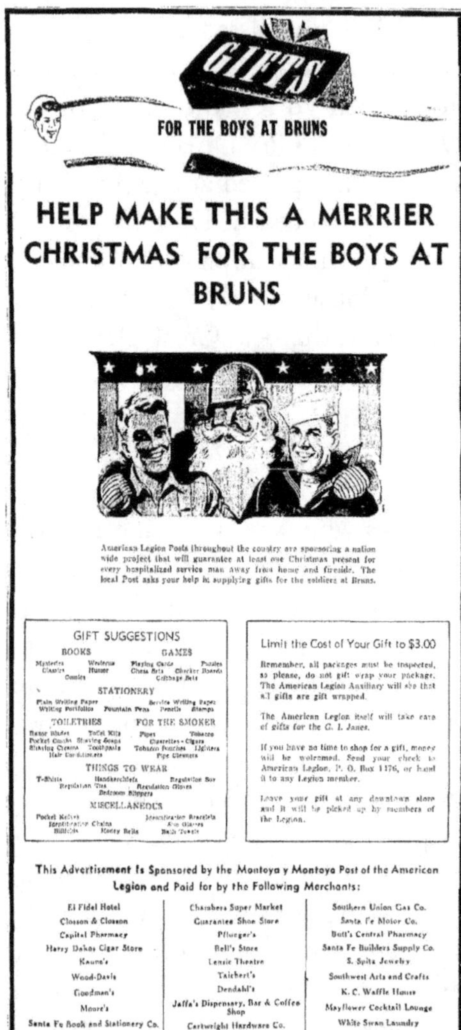

Figure 25. Advertisement for Bruns General Hospital. Three Greek-owned businesses, including the Mayflower Cocktail Lounge, are listed as sponsors. *Santa Fe New Mexican*, December 2, 1944.

Figure 26. Advertisement for Bruns General Hospital. Three Greek-owned businesses, including the Mayflower Cocktail Lounge, are listed as sponsors. *Santa Fe New Mexican*, November 21, 1944.

During the war, my father would drive our family to Las Vegas, New Mexico, about a one- or two-hour drive from Santa Fe at the time, to visit an uncle who had a farm there. On the way home, we would always stop and pick up hitchhiking soldiers, and bring them back to our house where my mother would make them a meal.

As a prominent restaurateur, my father Tom was well known. He would throw an annual Name Day celebration for himself every January. The Greeks never celebrate their birthdays, only their Name Days and every Greek is named after a Christian saint. The party in 1945 was particularly well attended, with 125 guests. Because of a snow storm, the one-day celebration stretched into two days, as reported in the *Santa Fe New Mexican* newspaper! Here is one photo of the party taken in the Pomonis living room. Tom Pomonis stands in the center with his left arm around his wife Helen's shoulder and his right arm around his brother's widow Carmen's shoulder (Fig. 27).

Figure 27. Father Sakellariou served in Albuquerque from October 1944 to June 30, 1949, so that helps date this photo. Probably Jan. 25, 1945 at Tom Pomonis' Name Day celebration. Photo in author's collection.

Top Row: Cecil Cleveland nee Tafoya (NM Sec. Of State, not Greek), Andy Gianatos ? , Steve Anthony, Efterpi Kalangis, Pete Theodore, ?, Waitress from Mayflower (not Greek), Esther Kartas, William Assimakis? ? (man peeking over on left)

Second Row: Gus Bruskas (bald), ? (man), ? (man), ? (woman), ? (woman), Presbytera Ethel Sakellariou, John Konis, Mrs/ Spondouris, Steve Spondouris, Georgia Kirikos, Tom Pomonis (host), Helen Pomonis (hostess and wife of Tom Pomonis), waitress (woman), Fanny Assimakis

Third Row: Father Sakellariou, Harry Dakos, Carmen Pomonis; on other side of Helen Pomonis is Vicki Rounesville, Edith Carellas, Gust Razatos

Fourth Row: Mike Kartas (man, mouth open), Hazel? (Mayflower waitress, not Greek), James George Pomonis (son of Tom and Helen Pomonis), Sarando Ike Kalangis, Pete Pomonis (son of Carmen Pomonis), Cornelia Kalangis, Mrs. Ades, George Ades, ? (man in uniform, Greek), ? (man smiling with mouth open)

Fifth Row: Katherine Pomonis (wearing white pinafore, daughter of Tom and Helen Pomonis), Diane Pomonis, William Kirikos (Diane's godfather), Barbara Pomonis, ? (man with glasses).

Tom Pomonis sold the Mayflower in 1952 after a prolonged strike (Fig. 28) to Evangelos Klonis. Tom passed in 1965 and Helen passed in 1986. Pete Pomonis passed in 1941.

May 14, 1950 SANTA FE NEW MEXICAN

HIS IS THE TRUTH—100 PER CENT COOPERATION

Photo of Mayflower Cafe employes and management, taken Thursday, May 11th

Angelo Klonis, part-owner of the Mayflower Cafe submits the following statement: "Since the union attempt to force organization of cafe employes started on Tuesday, May 9, not one of the employes of this restaurant has walked off the job. My employes are with our management 100 per cent. There has been no unrest among waitresses or other workers at our cafe.

"Present employes of this cafe do not wish to affiliate with any union, and they printed signs to that effect, which have been placed in the windows of the cafe, one of the largest in this city. Mary Asbury, an employe of the Mayflower for 10 years, said that she, oldest employe in point of service, did not wish 'under any circumstance' to join a union. Ruth Boggs, waitress at the Mayflower for four years, said, Speaking for all the waitresses at the Mayflower, we do not wish to join a union, and we do not want to be bothered any more by union organizers.' She added that working conditions at the Mayflower '. . . are the best, and the girls are completely happy with their pay and their treatment by the management.'

"Mary Bursey, for five years a waitress at the Mayflower, said that she had been approached on several occasions by union organizers but each time she had told them that she did not wish to join any union. 'I am completely satisfied with my position at the Mayflower, and the union can offer me no benefits that I do not receive under the present management at the Mayflower!'

"The average work week at the Mayflower is 48 hours. The waitresses and other employes work eight hours a day, six days a week, and are given their meals on company time. There is no charge made for meals of employes, and they eat their meals during their eight-hour shifts.

"The management of the Mayflower has always tried, and will continue to try to cooperate in every way with its employes. The employes of the Mayflower have always been able to discuss any problems concerning wages or working conditions with the owners of the Mayflower, and they will always be able to do so."

"The same conditions concerning union affiliation by employes are in effect at the Mayflower cocktail lounge, managed by Jerry Travalos. Mr. Travalos states his position as follows: 'This is a democratic country, and the question of joining a union or not joining a union is up to my employes.' No employes of the Mayflower Cocktail Lounge have been approached by union organizers, but the employes have announced they do not wish to join a union."

"We appreciate the patronage and cooperation of the residents of Santa Fe and the surrounding area. We shall always endeavor to treat our employes and customers with utmost courtesy, and we shall continue operations under the same policy that has been in effect--a policy which has made the Mayflower the meeting place of most of the people of Santa Fe.

GOOD FOOD—WELL SERVED

MAYFLOWER CAFE

ON THE PLAZA

Figure 28. In 1950, organizers attempted to unionize the Mayflower. Their efforts were opposed by the employees. The advertisement describes the working conditions at the café. *Santa Fe New Mexican*, May 14, 1950.

Pete Theodoratus, also known as Pete Theodore, was born in 1893 on the Greek island of Cephalonia. In 1942, Pete Theodore became a partner with the Pomonis brothers in the Mayflower Café on the Plaza and in the Mayflower Cocktail Room. Theodore started out in Gallup, New Mexico, where in 1931 he was a member of an American Hellenic Educational Progressive Association (AHEPA) chapter with fellow Greek George Ades, who was the first Mayor of Grants, New Mexico. In 1932, Theodore was not listed in the *Santa Fe City Directory*. But in 1934, he was listed as an owner of Candyland on Lincoln Avenue and of the Lensic Sandwich Shop on West San Francisco Street; and in 1936 and 1938, he was an owner of the Lensic Sandwich Shop. In 1936, he was a member of the new Hellenic American Voting Club in Santa Fe, but was still named as a member of the AHEPA Gallup Chapter. In 1940, he was not shown as an owner of any Santa Fe business. A December 24, 1940, Mayflower Café Christmas advertisement (Fig. 23) included greetings from Mr. and Mrs. Pete Theodore, but there is no evidence that he ever married. In 1945, he was proprietor of the Mayflower Cocktail Lounge. The Mayflower Cocktail Lounge, along with other Santa Fe Greek-owned businesses and other businesses, supported Bruns General Hospital during the holidays (Figs. 25, 26). Theodore appeared in the 1947 Santa Fe City Directory. He passed in 1949.

In 1945, fifteen years after the Pomonis brothers established the café in 1930, Angelos Spiros Klonis became a partner with Tom Pomonis in the Mayflower Café (Fig. 29). Klonis was born in 1916 in the village of Korgena on the Greek island of Cephalonia. In 1938, Klonis was a waiter at the Lensic Sandwich Shop. He did not appear in the 1940 *Santa Fe City Directory*. When he registered for the WWII draft, he stated that he was working at the KC Waffle House. He enlisted in the U.S. Armed Forces and fought in WWII. I remember after the war, my mother and I drove with him to Los Angeles to meet his future wife, Kiki. Klonis operated the Mayflower as a sole proprietor from 1952 after Tom Pomonis retired, to 1955 when the building was demolished. Klonis went on to establish Evangelo's Bar on West San Francisco Street in the location of the Faith Café.

Figure 29. Evangelos Klonis and Tom Pomonis, c. 1946 at the front counter of the Mayflower Café on the Plaza. Photo in author's collection.

Dennis (Dan) Vorres, brother of Helen Pomonis (wife of Tom Pomonis), was born in 1895 on the Greek island of Zakynthos. He immigrated in 1914. He registered for the WWI U.S. draft. He worked in 1930 as a gateman for the Chicago and Northwest Railroad and said he used to play cards with Al Capone. He worked as a cook at the Mayflower Café from at least 1940 to 1947, and in Gallup at the M&M Café in 1956 and the Manhattan Café in 1958. He passed in Santa Fe in 1964 at an apartment complex owned and managed by Tom Longas.

James Theofilas was a dishwasher at the Mayflower Café in 1930.

In 1940, Angelo Gallanais (Gallianos), and George Flongeris (Flendgeris) were listed as cooks at the Mayflower Café.

In 1940, Antonio (Tony, wife Grace) D. Chegaris (Chegarass, Chegarias) was a cook at the Mayflower Café. He was born in 1891 in Lykoudio,

Greece, immigrated in 1909, married a Greek woman named Maria in Los Angeles in 1929, and petitioned for naturalization in 1932. In 1940 he appeared in the Santa Fe City Directory, living alone and working as a cook. In the 1947 Santa Fe City Directory he appeared as a chef at the Mayflower Café, married to Grace who was born in 1890. Tony passed in 1976 and Grace passed in 1991.

Spiro (Sam) Fotopoulos (Fotoponolos) came in 1941 from Los Angeles to be the chef at the Mayflower Café. He appeared in the 1942 and 1944 Santa Fe City Directories. One night he left his apartment door unlocked and a burglar took money from his pants pocket and in the process dropped and broke his bridge which he kept in his pants pocket. By 1944, he had moved from his apartment and was a roomer at the home of the widow Eloisa Stewart. Stewart owned El Plato Sabroso at the same address of 214 College Street.

Nick Morris appeared in the 1920 and 1940 U.S. Censuses. He was born in 1891 in Greece and immigrated in 1911. In 1916 he married Eva Hudson of Albuquerque. In 1940, he and Eva were in Santa Fe where he worked as a cook at the Mayflower Café. According to a 1940 news article, he was a famous chef in Los Angeles and Tom Pomonis had brought him to the Mayflower Café at its 1940 reopening to work as head chef.

William Alafris appeared in the 1940 Santa Fe City Directory as a waiter at the Mayflower Café. In 1942, according to the Santa Fe City Directory, he had moved to the El Fidel Grill and had a wife named Ruby.

James Fillas and George Markis appeared in a 1940 Christmas Mayflower Café newspaper advertisement (Fig. 23), but otherwise did not appear in any Santa Fe City Directories or U.S. Censuses.

Tom Panage Yanatos in 1942 was a waiter at the Mayflower Café. He enlisted in the U.S. Armed Forces and served in WWII. He was born in 1897 in Manntgavinata, Greece, and was a stowaway to the United States in 1928. After his U.S. military service, he was arrested and deportation proceedings began. New Mexico Representative Fernandez then introduced a bill to grant Yanatos his citizenship, and in 1948 he was naturalized along with Dennis George Vorres. He worked at the Faith Café in the 1950's and passed in 1979.

Jerome "Jerry" (wife Lucille) Travlos worked at the Mayflower Cocktail Lounge from 1950 to at least 1953. By 1955 when the Mayflower ceased operating, he had moved to the Sombrero, a bar on Cerrillos Road. His wife Lucille was from Colorado and had lived in San Francisco, and her mother and father were from Greece. In the 1950 U.S. Census, Jerry and Lucille had living with them their daughter Joyce, and Lucille's mother Persephone Ganatos and Lucille's uncle Tom Monocrusos.

Andrew Ganatos of the Mayflower Cocktail Lounge was Lucille Travlos' brother.

As we continue down the street, we come to 62 ½ East San Francisco Street, the site of Goodman's Men's Store.

62 East San Francisco Street next door was the site of Wood-Davis Hardware.

Ilfeld Building

Our walk down East San Francisco Street now takes us to 60-58 East San Francisco Street. This was one of several Ilfeld buildings in Santa Fe.

60 East San Francisco Street was the site of the Santa Fe Chocolate Shop. In 1923 Gust Razatos and Pete Regos (Rigas) bought The Bank, a confectionary, which had been open since at least 1919 (Fig. 30). They closed it and remodeled it, and renamed it the Santa Fe Chocolate Shop (Fig. 31). Or rather, the new proprietors did something that was fashionable at the time in Santa Fe: they held a contest to name their new business, and 12-year old Florence May won the ten dollar gold piece.

By 1928 Regos apparently sold his share to Lee Diamantis, who appeared in the 1928 City Directory but never appeared in it again. From 1932 to 1934, Regos owned the Trail Pig Stand Café on Cerrillos Road.

By 1930, the Chocolate Shop was owned by Gust Razatos, Antonio Pino, and William Assimakis (alternate spellings: Arimakis, Asamakis, Asimakis, Cissimakis). By 1932, the shop was owned by Pino, and Mike Keros (father of Thee Keros). By 1934, Pino and Keros had opened a second shop down the street at 127 West San Francisco. By 1936 the two shops were closed and 60-58 East San Francisco Street became a Woolworth's and 127 West San Francisco became Kahn's Shoe Store.

Konstantinos "Gus(t)" G. Razatos, known locally as Cuchillo, was born in 1886 in Greece and immigrated in 1906. In the 1920 U.S. Census, Gust Razatos was a lodger (that is, apparently unrelated or distantly related) with Spiros Razatos in Denver. Spiros Razatos appeared in the 1920 Denver City Directory as proprietor of Denver Candy Company. Gust came to Santa Fe after the 1920 U.S. Census but before 1923. Gust originally lived at 230 or 290 West San Francisco Street, but became a long-time resident of the Plaza Hotel. He appeared in the 1930 U.S. Census in Santa Fe but not in the 1940 U.S. Census. He appeared as a defendant in a 1947 lawsuit in Santa Fe. In the 1947 Santa Fe City Directory he owned the Package Liquor Store and still lived at the Plaza Hotel. He passed in 1949.

Figure 30.
Advertisement for The Bank (a confectionary).
Santa Fe New Mexican, March 2, 1923.

Figure 31.
Advertisement for the Santa Fe Chocolate Shop.
Santa Fe New Mexican, April 15, 1923.

58 East San Francisco Street in 1934 was occupied by Economy Shoe Shop. By 1936, 60-58 East San Francisco Street was now occupied by F W Woolworth.

56 East San Francisco Street next door was occupied by Zook's Pharmacy (Fig. 32).

Figure 32. Advertisement for Zook's Pharmacy. Santa Fe New Mexican. June 2, 1933.

Spitz Building

We now come to 54 ½ East San Francisco Street and the Spitz Building. It was occupied by a lawyer, by Builder's Materials, and by the Independent Order of Odd Fellows Hall.

We continue to 54 East San Francisco Street which was occupied by Kaune Grocers.

50 East San Francisco Street was occupied by Beacham-Mignardot Hardware.

52-50 East San Francisco Street by 1936 was occupied by JC Penny.

2
A LEFT TURN ON LINCOLN AVENUE

Here we backtrack slightly to make a left turn, north, on Lincoln Avenue along the west side of the Plaza (Map 3, Fig. 33). On the sidewalk ahead of you, you can see the overflow seating for the current Plaza Café.

The first Plaza Café opened July 23, 1913 on the west side of the Plaza at an undetermined address (Fig. 34). The next year on Nov. 23, 1914, it was bought and reopened by "Economou & Bachis" (Figs. 35, 36).

A year after that, on October 15, 1915, Bachis (there is no mention of Economou) moved the Plaza Café to the Metropolitan Hotel (formerly La Salle Hotel owned by Charley Gann) on 241 San Francisco Street and renamed it the Metropolitan Café (Figs. 37-39) (The address locations might have changed since 1915 because the 200 block of East San Francisco Street is not near the southwest corner of the Plaza as indicated in the 1913 advertisement for La Salle.). Apparently, the Metropolitan Hotel didn't stay open for more than a year or so.

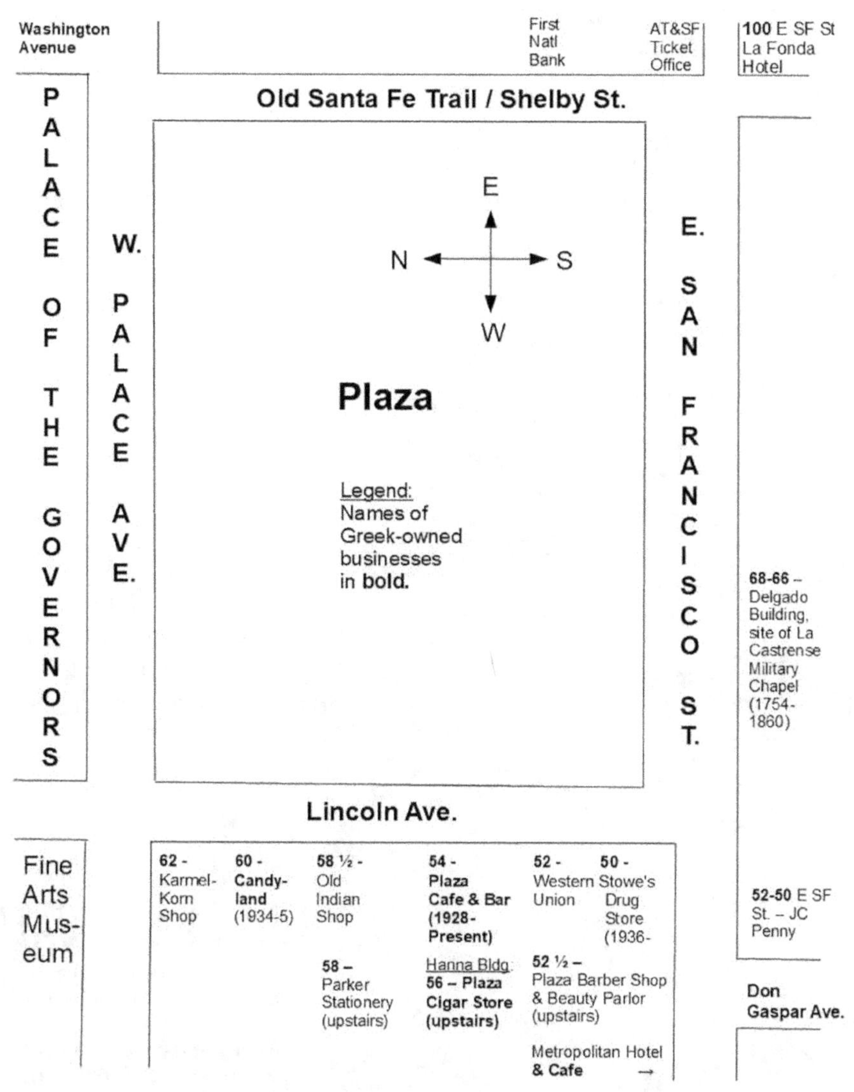

Map 3. Lincoln Avenue.

WHITE  SWAN

LAUNDRY — PHONE 840

CLEANERS, DYERS, HATTERS — TAILORS, FURRIERS

320

Stop at a HILTON HOTEL

ALBUQUERQUE
EL PASO
PLAINVIEW
LUBBOCK
LONGVIEW
ABILENE
LONG BEACH
San Francisco (SIR FRANCIS DRAKE)

"You pay no more for the best at a Hilton"

KEARNEY AV—(Cont'd)
123 Martinez Alfredo ⓒ
124 Silva Luciano
125 Benavides Atanacio
126 Trujillo Quirino ⓒ
127 Padilla Octaviano ⓒ
128 Ortiz C P

LAS VEGAS HIGHWAY
Begins 806 College ext south (Right Even)
911 Urioste T B Mrs ⓒ
913 Lopez R G serv sta
913½ Leyva Luciano
Lopez R G
Coronado rd intersects
1002△Viera A T Mrs ⓒ
ws△Sebastian C R ⓒ
ws△Santa Fe Armory
ws△Chase E P ⓒ

LAUGHLIN
Begins 645 Don Gaspar av ext west

LA VEREDA
Begins 729 E Palace av ext northeast in semi-circle (Right Odd)
112△Officer R M
118△Ortiz P G ⓒ
120 **Renehan Apts**
*1△Murphy L T
*2△Renehan Marietta Mrs ⓒ
*3 Werb B W Jr
*4 Phillips Eliz
*6 Dempster Genevieve Mrs
*7△Magers H B
*8△Dilworth S J
*9△Ballow I W Jr
*10△Mandell H N
*11△Neblett Colin
*12△Greer H K

LINCOLN
West side of Plaza begins San Francisco ext north (Right Odd)
50△Stowe's Drug Store
Stowe's Beauty Salon
52△Western Union Tel Co
52½ Plaza Barber Shop
Plaza Beauty Shop
54△Plaza Cafe
54½ **Hanna Bldg**
△Flores Studio
△Clodfelter M L chiro
56△Plaza Cigar Store
58½△Old Indian Shop
60△Don's Sptg Gds Co
Myrick's Red Saddle Shop
62△Vic's Dispensary
Children's Cafe
Dalbey Peggy Hosiery—Lingerie

Palace av intersects
111-13△Elks Home
116△Hewett E L
116-20△Wood-Davis Hdw Co
119 Vacant
121△Cash Hazel Bar
125△Montgomery Ward & Co order office
126△Foster Joseph phys
127△N M Office Sup Co
129△Town & Country Shop clo
131△Maytag Shop
133△Batrite Pastry Shop
135△Batrite Food Stores
136△Doll C E ⓒ
142△Hart H E
142½ Myers J A
143△Livingston I S Mrs ⓒ
Marcy intersects
203△Nuding F E ⓒ
207△Hase Anna L
211△Goutchey J J ⓒ
214△Catron School
215-17 Watterson E D
219△Nunlist F F
225△Gans Julius ⓒ
Federal pl intersects

LLANO LARGO
Begins Sunset 1 blk n of Artist ext northeast
100△Lumpkins W T ⓒ

LOLITA
Begins 821 Hickox ext north (Right Odd)
510 Baca Lorenzo
515 de Baca A C ⓒ
516 Garcia F A ⓒ
517 Cordova Agapito ⓒ
520 Roybal Eugenio
rear Romero Camilo ⓒ
521 Alarid Santiago
525 Sandoval Pablo ⓒ
526 Ulivarri Fulgencio ⓒ
527 Barela Lorenzo ⓒ

LOPEZ
Begins 856 Dunlap ext west (Right Odd)
903 Quintana Jose
906 Cruz Victoriano ⓒ
910 Gonzalez Abran ⓒ
914 Ortiz Max ⓒ
915 Padilla Arcenia Mrs
916 Gomez Victor
918 Gonzalez Hilario ⓒ
rear Duran Teodoro
922 Brendle R F
930 Telles Lucas ⓒ
934 Vigil Pablo
940 Carrillo Emilia Mrs ⓒ
942 Sanchez Manuelita Mrs
948 Gonzalez Nicolas ⓒ

Figure 33. Page from Hudspeth's 1940 Santa Fe City Directory showing the businesses on Lincoln Avenue.

THE PLAZA CAFE

This is a new place to eat, and will prove a delightful surprise to everybody. Clean and wholesome food and the best service assured. Come and get acquainted with Santa Fe's New Restaurant. Large, airy and comfortable rooms in connection. All the modern improvements.

THE PLAZA CAFE

West Side of Plaza.

SANTA FE, - - - NEW MEXICO

Figure 34. Advertisement for the first Plaza Café. *Santa Fe New Mexican*, July 24, 1913.

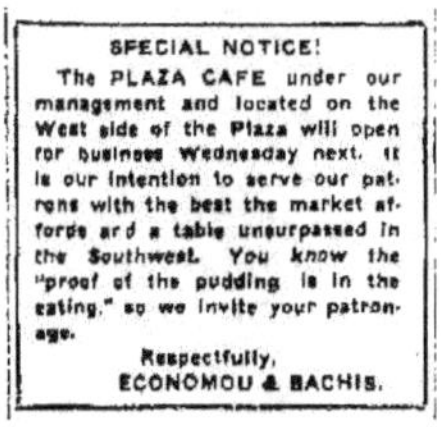
SPECIAL NOTICE!
The PLAZA CAFE under our management and located on the West side of the Plaza will open for business Wednesday next. It is our intention to serve our patrons with the best the market affords and a table unsurpassed in the Southwest. You know the "proof of the pudding is in the eating," so we invite your patronage.
Respectfully,
ECONOMOU & BACHIS.

Figure 35. Advertisement for the first Plaza Café. *Santa Fe New Mexican*, Nov. 21, 1914.

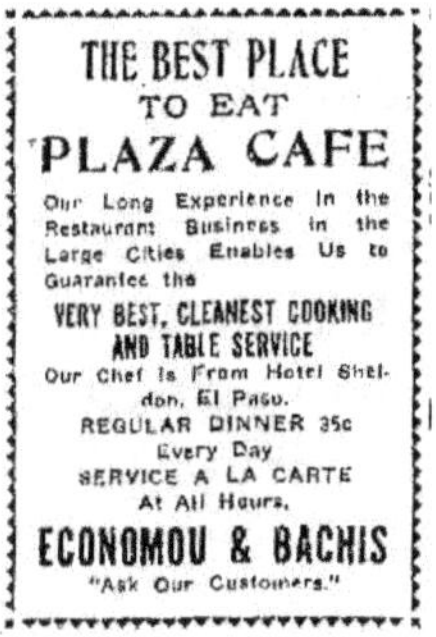
THE BEST PLACE
TO EAT
PLAZA CAFE
Our Long Experience in the Restaurant Business in the Large Cities Enables Us to Guarantee the
VERY BEST, CLEANEST COOKING
AND TABLE SERVICE
Our Chef is From Hotel Sheldon, El Paso.
REGULAR DINNER 35c
Every Day
SERVICE A LA CARTE
At All Hours.
ECONOMOU & BACHIS
"Ask Our Customers."

Figure 36. Advertisement for the first Plaza Café. *Santa Fe New Mexican*, Dec. 9, 1914.

La Salle Hotel
CHARLEY GANN, Prop'r
European Plan.
Meals At All Hours.
Elegant Rooms in Connection. Steam Heat,
Electric Lights and Baths.
RATES: 50c and 75c PER DAY.
241 San Francisco Street,
Near S. W. Corner Plaza,

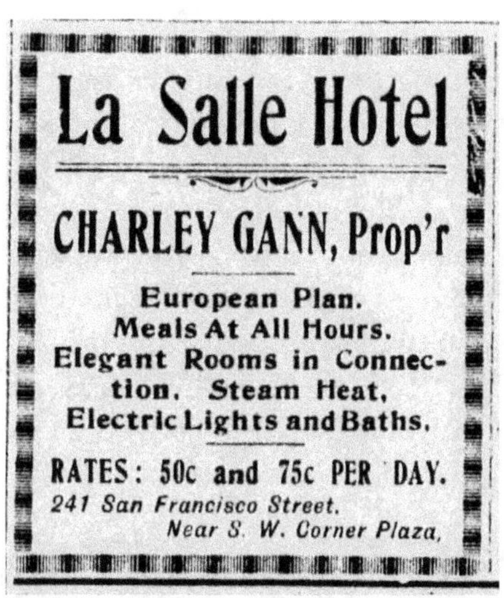

Figure 37. Advertisement for La Salle Hotel. *Santa Fe New Mexican*, June 14, 1913.

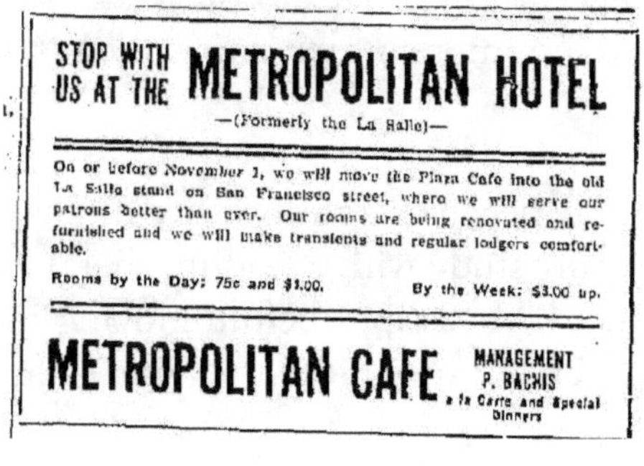
STOP WITH US AT THE
METROPOLITAN HOTEL
—(Formerly the La Salle)—
On or before November 1, we will move the Plaza Cafe into the old La Salle stand on San Francisco street, where we will serve our patrons better than ever. Our rooms are being renovated and refurnished and we will make transients and regular lodgers comfortable.
Rooms by the Day: 75c and $1.00.
By the Week: $3.00 up.
METROPOLITAN CAFE
MANAGEMENT
P. BACHIS
a la Carte and Special Dinners

Figure 38. Advertisement for the Metropolitan Hotel. *Santa Fe New Mexican*, Oct. 12, 1915.

BUILDING ENTRANCE CHANGED

Changes are being made to the front entrance of the building on San Francisco street recently vacated by the Metropolitan cafe. The building is to be occupied soon by the Art Shop, which lost its home in the recent fire.

Figure 39.
Notice on the Metropolitan Hotel.
Santa Fe New Mexican, Dec. 29, 1917.

That's the background. Now, 54 Lincoln Avenue became the site of the second Plaza Café. James (wife Anastasia) and Spiros Ipiotis, and Stephen (Steve) Karman (wife Georgia), opened the Plaza Café on Feb. 22, 1928 (Fig. 40). Steve Karman had been in Santa Fe since at least 1928, and apparently had a sister Eva living with him in 1932. He married Georgia in 1934. The new Plaza Café of 1928 had nothing to do with the old Plaza Café of 1913–1915. This new café was located at the site of the Eagle Café in the Hanna Building.

The Plaza Café was remodeled in 1941, at which time Harry Dakos (wife Bernice/Betty, second wife Vasso) was running the Plaza Tap Room (Fig. 41). By 1942, the Tap Room was known as the Plaza Cocktail Lounge.

In 1944, the proprietors of the Plaza Café were Stelios (Steve) Anthony and George Nikolis, while James and Spiros Ipiotis, and Steve Anthony, were proprietors of the Plaza Cocktail Lounge. James Ipiotis' son Ted owned the Plaza Cigar Store, but Harry Dakos also appeared as an owner of both the Cocktail Lounge (Tap Room) and the Cigar Store. Steve Anthony had just divorced and sold his share in the Faith Café on West San Francisco Street to his partner Alex Kalangis.

Steve Anthony was born in 1896 in Greece. He immigrated in 1916. Anthony appeared in the 1930 U.S. Census as a farmer in Hagerman, Chaves County, New Mexico. He opened the Faith Café on West San Francisco Street in 1934. We will discuss him more in that entry. By 1940 he was naturalized.

James Ipiotis was born 1891 in Greece. He began as a dishwasher in New York City and saved his money to eventually study with a leading chef. He opened his first restaurants in Indiana and Mississippi before moving to Santa Fe, where he bought the Eagle Café and changed it to the Plaza Café. He passed in 1982.

Spiros or Saiomas Ipiotis was born in 1893 in Greece. He operated the Plaza Cocktail Lounge up to his passing. Spiros served in the Balkan Wars from 1912 to 1914 and came to the United States after WWI. He and his brother came from Mytilene on the island of Lesbos, Greece. Spiros passed in 1960.

Harry Dakos was born in 1898 as Haralampos Daskalos. He was naturalized in 1934 and changed his name to Harry Dakos. Dakos previously operated the bar at the Elks Club. He passed in 1959.

George (wife Helen) Nikolis was an owner of the Plaza Café in 1947.

In 1947 the Plaza Café was bought by Dan Razatos. Dan Razatos was born in 1909 or 1910 on the island of Cephalonia, Greece. His uncle was Spiros Razatos of Denver. Dan Razatos first appeared in the Santa Fe City Directory in 1937 as a proprietor, with Ted Otero, of the Santa Fe Fruit Market. We discuss this business in the chapter on Galisteo Street.

In 1938 Razatos was proprietor of the California Fruit Market at Water and Agua Fria (224 Water Street). In 1941 he was still at Water Street and was divorced from Phyrne. He was not in the 1944 or 1947 Santa Fe City Directories. By 1948 he was proprietor of the Plaza Café with Dan Pomonis, who had been a miner at Crosby, Wyoming, as were my father and uncle Tom and Pete Pomonis. In 1952, Dan Razatos opened the Dover Circus and Rustic Lounge and Bar at 623 Cerrillos Road, with George Peros. In 1953 he took Phil Pomonis (son of Dan Pomonis) as a partner in the Plaza Café, and also joined Lester Phillips at the Handy Way Liquor Store at 529 Cerrillos Rd. In 1961 he married Bene and they had four children together. In 1997 he passed away.

Daniel Poulos and Gus Tsolakis were waiters at the Plaza Café in 1928.

Athanasius (Athan, Arthur) Meimary was a cook at the Plaza Café in 1930. Athan was born in 1889 in Turkey, immigrated in 1907, and was naturalized in 1926. He appeared in the 1930 U.S. Census, single and living in Arthur and Ada Robinson's rooming house at 122 Grant Avenue. Also living at the boarding house, according to the U.S. Census, was a naturalized Greek miner named Sam J. Brown. In 1936, as discussed in

Chapter 10, Athan and a Gust Meimary were proprietors of the Bar-B-Q Stand and were living at Orchard Camp.

Gus Palus, a WWI U.S. veteran, was a waiter at the Plaza Café in 1950. By 1955 he was a bartender at the Yucca Bar on De Vargas.

February 21, 1928 SANTA FE NEW MEXICAN Page Three

THE PLAZA CAFE

Announces their Formal Opening

11 A. M., WEDNESDAY, FEBRUARY 22, 1928

SPECIAL ENTERTAINMENT
Will be Provided for this Occasion

Flowers for Every Lady Visitor
Cigars for the Gentlemen

Hear Our New Panatrope

OPEN DAY AND NIGHT

Menu

—SOUP—
Choice of
Chicken a la Royal or Turkey Broth with Rice
—RELISHES—
Head Lettuce Thousand Island Dressing
—CHOICE OF MEATS—
Roast Young Turkey
With Chestnut Dressing and Cranberry Sauce
Long Island Young Duck
With Celery Dressing and Green Apple Sauce
Stuffed Young Chicken—Sage Dressing
Fricassee of Chicken with Egg Noodles
Roast Extra Cut of Beef au Jus
Roast Loin of Pork, Apple Sauce
Roast Young Spring Lamb with Jelly
—VEGETABLES—
Au Gratin Cauliflower
Green June Peas Drawn in Butter
White Snowflake Potatoes
—DESSERT—
Home Made Pumpkin Pie with Whipped Cream
Vanilla Ice Cream with Home Made Cake
—DRINKS—
Coffee Milk Cocoa Hot Tea
SOLANA FARM PASTEURIZED MILK AND CREAM

The most Modern Cafe in the entire Southwest will soon be open to the public

The Homelike Atmosphere of our establishment will appeal to everyone and the appetizing way in which our foods are prepared and served will please the most fastidious

Our Foods are more than just pure ---they are tasty and different!

DROP IN AFTER THE SHOW OR AFTER THE DANCE

Figure 40.
Advertisement for the Plaza Café, *Santa Fe New Mexican*, Feb. 21, 1928.

Figure 41. Advertisement for the Plaza Café, *Santa Fe New Mexican*, Apr. 11, 1941.

Further down the street at 60 Lincoln Avenue was Candyland, a confectionary, opened in 1934 by Pete Theodore, William Assimakis, and Pete Columbus. By 1936 it was closed.

William (wife Fannie) Assimakis (alternative spellings Arimakis, Asamakis, Cissimakis), confectioner, appeared in the 1920 U.S. Census for Santa Fe as a laborer in a lumber camp. He was born in 1895 and immigrated from Greece in 1899. In 1920 he lived in a hotel at 158 Don Gaspar. The address did not exist in the 1928 City Directory, which is our earliest directory, but there was the Motezuma Hotel at 120 Don Gaspar, so the numbering might have changed. He later lived in the Capital Hotel at 236 Montezuma. He was a partner in the Santa Fe Chocolate Shop from 1930-31, a partner in Candyland from 1934-35, and was at the El Fidel Grill from 1936-37. Along with him, his wife Fannie appeared in the 1940 U.S. Census with daughters Georgia (8) and Patricia (6). He passed away in 1957 in Albuquerque.

When Candyland closed in 1936, co-owner Pete (wife Lula) Antonio Columbus (Columbis) became a cook at the Faith Café. Columbus was born in 1882 in Sparta, Greece, registered for the WWII draft while living in Holbrook, Arizona (he might be the same Pete Columbus who registered for the WWI draft in Georgia), and passed in 1953.

3
MAKING SENSE OF SANTA FE: THE LAWS OF THE INDIES

One reason my Greek parents moved to Santa Fe was because it reminded them of the homeland they had left. They used to say that the Santa Fe Plaza in particular reminded them of the plazas in Greece. Because the Santa Fe Plaza had such an influence on the Greeks' decisions to stay in Santa Fe, I would like to take a few pages to discuss the historical origin and importance of the Plaza. What motivated my parents and the other Greeks to stay was not dry history but a feeling of beauty and a coming together of the community. I cannot capture that for you but I can explain how the Plaza and the Palace had their origins in the Laws of the Indies.

The Laws of the Indies were laws on town planning issued in 1573 by King Phillip II of Spain. These Laws were to accompany all expeditions to the New World. They dictated that the location, layout, form and settlement patterns were to be as follows (Fig. 42):

The plaza, also known as Plaza de armas, was to be one-and-one-half times long as wide in order to accommodate fiestas and military drills of men mounted on horses.

The Cathedral was to be sited on elevated ground.
Government buildings, or las Casas Reales, which included the governor's housing and the Presidio or military fort, was to be sited along the north side of the Plaza.

Sidewalks were to be sheltered by portales (portals).
The area must be fertile and have abundant water.

The first Law of the Indies dealt with the Plaza de armas. The Plaza was "designed for military and religious functions and is to be constructed at least half again as long as its width, as this form is best for celebrations with horses." The Santa Fe Plaza was eventually shortened.

Two archaeologists, Bruce Ellis and Cordelia Snow, speculated that the Plaza originally extended as far east as St. Francis Cathedral and was four times its present size and extended south down to Water Street. In 1990, archaeologists excavated the Plaza to see what it had been back in 1610. These archaeologists were given the Cowchip Award because they discovered through this excavation that it had been a plaza.

The second Law of the Indies dealt with the church. The first church of the Plaza, La Parroquia or parish church, was built east of the Plaza from 1622-26. The church's plan and location are unknown but it is believed to have stood immediately behind the present Cathedral, facing west as the Cathedral does today. The second Parroquia contained the statue of La Conquistadora or Lady of Conquest, which can be seen today in the north wing of the Cathedral which is also the only remaining portion of La Parroquia.

Another church, San Miguel Mission, was built in 1626 and was used as a parish church to serve the religious needs of the Indian laborers brought from Mexico. It was located in the Barrio de Analco south of the Santa Fe River. Analco is the Tlascalan Indian word for "other side of the river." It is now considered Santa Fe's oldest neighborhood. This was the first section of Santa Fe to be sacked and razed during the Pueblo Revolt of 1680.

The third Law of the Indies dealt with the Casas Reales or royal house. It included the Palace of the Governors, where the governor's private apartments, official reception room, and the office and servants' quarters were located. It also included the Presidio where the troops were garrisoned, and the stables and arsenal. The Casas Reales also contained a vegetable garden of ten acres, and two torreones or defensive towers, one used as a prison and storage for gunpowder, and the other as a chapel.

It is not known what the Casas Reales really looked like because the Pueblo Revolt of 1680 resulted in the destruction of virtually every locally generated scrap of paper documenting everyday life in New Mexico. Any physical description of the Plaza between 1610 and 1680 has been pieced together from only fragmentary evidence based on correspondence sent to Mexico and Spain, post-re-conquest recollections, and scant archaeological evidence.

The fourth Law of the Indies dealt with the portales.

The fifth Law of the Indies dealt with the selection of a site for villas. This was to be based, among other things, on the abundance of drinking and irrigation water.

The Santa Fe River flows freely down the Sangre de Cristo Mountains through the Santa Fe Canyon. In past years, this river overflowed its banks and created flood plains.

According to David H. Snow, colonists and Pueblo Indian conscripts dug two acequia madres—otherwise known as mother irrigation ditches - in order to water fields on either side of the river. There may have been as many as 38 branches from these two acequias.

Lacking references to Santa Fe's acequias prior to 1680, we can only guess at their locations and courses. However, it can be argued that the north ditch supplied the Plaza and its administrative and military compound, the Parroquia or parish church, and the settlers' fields and gardens adjacent to the Plaza.

Cienega is Spanish for marsh or swamp or wetland. There were cienegas found in several areas of the villas. The water table was known to be high in early Santa Fe. Today there is a street three blocks east of the Plaza off Palace Avenue that is called Cienega Street in the same location of the Santa Fe cienega. This wetland may have been the source of the acequia—possibly now Marcy Street - that led into the Casas Reales. This acequia was cut off by the Indians during the Pueblo Revolt of 1680, leaving the colonists and their cattle without water and forcing them to flee. It may have also been the water source that De Vargas cut off in 1693 at the reconquest, allowing him to take back the Palace from the Indians. The cienega, or Arias Pond, was located higher than the surrounding area, so it may have also drained into Bishop Lamy's garden behind the Parroquia.

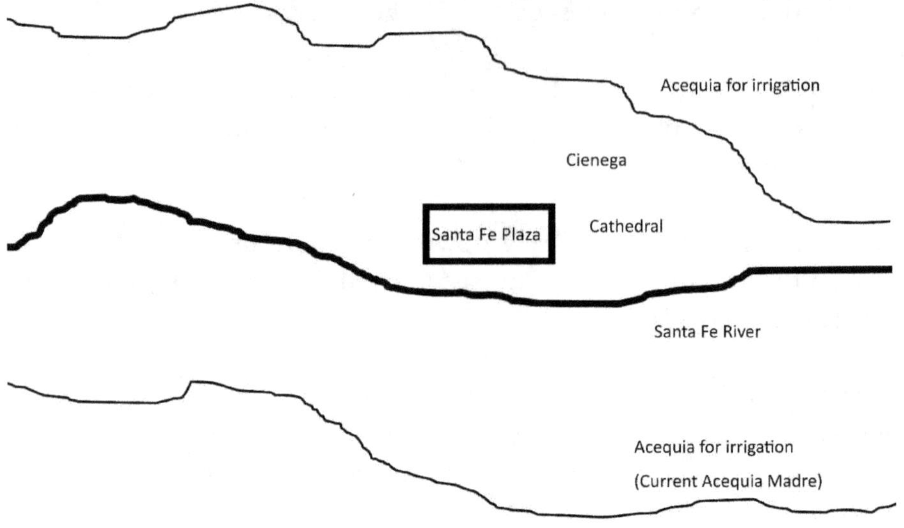

Figure 42. Idealized view from the earliest map of Santa Fe, drawn in 1766 by Second Lieutenant José Urrutia. North is at the top of the page.

4
THE PALACE AND THE PRESIDIO

The Law of the Indies required a Presidio, and the Palace of the Governors was part of that Presidio. However, by 1760, Bishop Tamarón of Durango, on a visit to Santa Fe, noted that there was no formal Presidio building remaining. The earliest map of Santa Fe, drawn in 1766 by Second Lieutenant José Urrutia (Fig. 42), does not show the Presidio! His southern acequia para regadio (irrigation ditch) is possibly the bed of the current acequia madre (mother ditch), as the northern one no longer exists.

Sixteen years later, in 1776, Fray Francisco Atanasio Dominguez, described the mournful appearance of the villas. He also noted that the fields, gardens and orchards were irrigated with water from acequias from the Santa Fe River or from cienegas or marshes east of the Plaza.

By 1780, officers of the Santa Fe Company were concerned with the inadequacy of the governmental buildings, or Casas Reales, which you now know includes the Governor's housing and the Presidio. These officers pledged 2,175 pesos from their retirement fund for construction of government buildings. However, there were many years of delays due to the Viceroy's late approval and a shortage of funds. In 1788, eight years later, the lumber project for the Presidio had been cut and stacked, and straw had been collected for the fabrication of the adobes. At last, approval came from the Viceroy, and Governor de la Concha called upon all unemployed settlers between the ages of fourteen and fifty to present themselves as wage laborers. Construction started in 1789. By 1791, construction again was delayed due to several months of heavy rain, which ruined some eighty thousand adobe bricks. Nevertheless, construction was completed that year. In 1982, archaeologists excavating behind the Palace found a thick layer of sand. They believed it was related to the massive summer storm in 1791 that destroyed the 80,000 adobe bricks. They also speculated that the finds from this excavation were related to the construction of the new Spanish Presidio completed in 1791.

Juan de Pagazaurtundua, a military engineer in Chihuahua City, drew up a plan of this second Presidio from specifications provided by people familiar with its construction (Fig. 43). This Presidio extended nearly a quarter of a mile north of the Plaza to where the present Federal Building is now located. As mentioned above, during the Spanish Colonial era, an acequia or irrigation ditch ran northwest from the Santa Fe River and curved around into the military compound behind the Palace. This was possibly the acequia that was cut off by the Indians and subsequently cut off by De Vargas at the time of the reconquest.

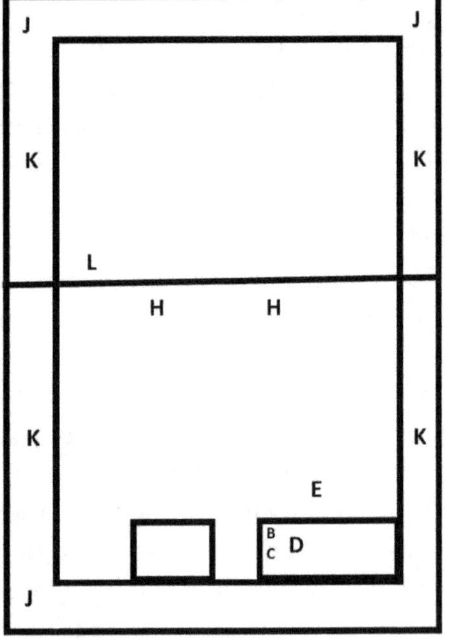

Figure 43. The plan of the second Presidio from Juan de Pagazaurtundua's 1791 reconstruction. North is up. The structure extends approximately from Washington Avenue to Grant Avenue, and from Palace Avenue to Federal Place. The single entrance to the entire complex was on the south side facing the Plaza. The plan shows an irrigation ditch (conductos de agua, L). Could this be the Casas Reales acequia of 1680 running through the middle of the compound? Laundries (labraderos, H) were situated on this ditch (this ditch is now possibly Marcy Street). An adobe wall surrounded the Presidio. Surrounding the interior compound were a little over one hundred quarters for the troops (K), with their respective corrals. The sergeant's quarters (J) were in the northwest, northeast and southwest corners. A garden (E) was north of the governor's residence, or the Palace (D). A guard room (B) and a jail (C) were attached to the west side of the residence. NOTE: These last two rooms were later removed to make room for Lincoln Avenue.

5
SAN FRANCISCO STREET, FROM LINCOLN AVENUE WESTWARD

We now backtrack our steps on Lincoln Avenue and return to East San Francisco Street, where the last business we looked at was JC Penny. On East San Francisco Street we walk westward to the next intersection which is Don Gaspar Avenue (Map 4, Figs. 44, 45).

Don Gaspar Avenue divides some major downtown thoroughfares into East and West sections, including San Francisco Street. We are now standing at the division of East and West San Francisco Street. East San Francisco Street is a short street, extending from where we are standing, east to the Cathedral. West San Francisco Street is longer.

The 100 block of West San Francisco Street begins at Don Gaspar Avenue and extends west to Galisteo Street. The 200 block of West San Francisco Street extends west from Galisteo Street to Sandoval Street. The 300 block extends west from Sandoval Street to North Guadalupe Street. Odd number addresses are on the north side of the street, on your right, and even number addresses are on the south side of the street, on your left.

100-102 West San Francisco Street, at the southwest corner of West San Francisco Street and Don Gaspar Avenue, was Santa Fe Book and Stationery.

114 West San Francisco Street on your left or the south side of the street was the site of Pay Less Drug Store. In 1940, Louis J. Peppers (Pepperis) opened Louis' Flower Shop (Fig. 46) in Pay Less Drug Store. In 1944, Peppers moved the shop around the corner to the Hotel El Fidel at 202-204 Galisteo Street, where he operated it through 1953.

117 West San Francisco Street, across the street and on your right or the north side of the street, was the site of the Mission Pool Hall. From 1932 to 1933 it was owned by Gust Razatos and Gust Daskalos.

Lincoln Ave.

Legend:
Names of
Greek-owned
businesses
in **bold.**

117 – Mission Pool Hall (1932-33)

121 – Paris Popcorn & Candy Shop (1938-1947), **Mitchell's Music** (1949-1959)
123 – Paris Theatre (1914-1948)

127 – Santa Fe Chocolate Shop (1934-1936)
127 ½ – Santa Fe Candy Kitchen (1938-1965)

201 – Candelario's Trading Post (1803-present)
203 – La Mariposa Bar (1946)

205 – Mitchell's Army Store (1949-1959), **Mitchell's Music** (1947-49)

Burro Alley

209 – Lensic Sandwich Shop (1934-1941)
211 – Lensic Theatre (1931-present)
213 – Lensic Dispensary (bar, 1942-1943)

W. SAN FRANCISCO ST.

50 – Beacham-Mignardot Hardware, later JC Penny (1936, #52-50)

Don Gaspar Ave.

100-102 – Santa Fe Book & Stationery

E
N S
W

114 – Louis' Flower Shop (in Payless Drug Store, 1940-1944)

Galisteo St.

200 W. SF St. / 106 Galisteo – **Faith Cafe** (1934-1964), later: **Evangelo's Bar** (1965-present)

210 – Burro Alley Cafe / Liquor (1940-1958+) (and Theatre)
212 – Coney Island Cafe (1932-1939)
214 – Burro Alley Cigar Store (1944-1954)
216 – Chili King Cafe (1940-1960)

Map 4. West San Francisco Street.

Figure 44. Page from Hudspeth's 1936 Santa Fe City Directory showing the businesses on West San Francisco Street. This can be compared to the 1940 City Directory shown below.

AN FRANCISCO E—Cont'd
Masonic Building
½△Spitz Jewelry Store &
Gift Shop
Gans Building
Rooms—
4△Maldonado Jose
△Resettlement Admin
7△Wolfe E F
△Broaddus W H
△Warn F R
10△Professional Exch
11 Amer Natl Ins Co
△Olsen Clara H
12-14△Barker C B
15△Harvey J C
16-17△Williams D R
18△Resettlement Admin
Street Continued
△Southwest Arts & Crafts
2△Capital Pharmacy
T W A
Varney Air Transport
△Blatt Inc
Blatt Beauty Shop
101-3△A T & S F Ry
105△Tohill N M
107△Dorman H H
109△Mack Photo Service
111△Lathrop A S
Van Atta Laboratories
111△Fiske F W
111½△Seth J O
△Montgomery A K
115△Spanish & Ind Trad Co
115½△New Mexico State
Record
122 St Francis Paroch Sch
123△Postoffice
Cathedral pl intersects

SAN FRANCISCO WEST
South side of Plaza begins at Don Gaspar av extends west and divides intersecting streets into north and south
50-2△Santa Fe Book & S Co
54½△**Laughlin Building**
Rooms—
3-4△Mera F E
5-6△Rolls J A
7-8△Claffey F J
9-12△Bowman H S
△Hill R J
△Mell J D
Graham Simplex Pump Co
16-17△N M Motor Transport
Assn
Harris Dan Ins Agcy
Commercial Casualty Ins
Co
Farmers Auto Inter Ins
Exch
Lumbermen's Under-
writers Alliance

*18-23△Barton W C
*24-28△Backer & McGinnis
*26△Associated Contrs of N M
*27 Neel Geo M
Street Continued
103 **Renehan Building**
Rooms—
*2△Lord D D
*8△Espe Ins & Surety Co
*313 Dieman C A
*316△Thomas B M
*317-20△Gilbert & Hamilton
*321△Staplin & Staplin
*326 Clodfelter M L
Street continued
105½△Hymel Dispensary
106△Yontz H C Jewelry Store
106½Pflueger John
107△Little Shop The
△Postal Tel Cable Co
108△Jahnke Emil
109△Mugler Millinery Shop
109½**Salmon Building**
Rooms—
*1-2△McIntosh C R
*3-4△Remley G E
*5-7△Kiker & Sanchez
U S Commr
*9-11△Chavez David Jr
Carmody D W
*12-19△Dem State Hdqtrs
*13△Prudential Ins Co
Jerns John & Co
*14-15△Holloman Reed
*20-22△Lujan-Moss Agcy
Montoya A A
Duran Victor
*25 Wilcox A B
*29 Salazar Celina
*30 Anderson Roy
*32-33 Smith Guthrie
*34 Mahboub Frank
Street Continued
110△Ballard's
111△Butt's Central Pharmacy
111△Emporium Inc
112△Taichert's Variety Store
113△O K Barber Shop
114△Bells Store Inc
115△Popular The
117△Spouse-Reitz Co Inc
118△Field Chas Co
119△Bank Bar
120 **Galisteo Building**
2d fl△N M State & Natl
Re-emp Serv
120½Vacant
121 Paris News Stand
121½△Laughlin Frank
122△Beer's Ready-to-Wear
123△Paris Theatre
123½Paris Shoe Shine Parlor
125△New Mex Cafe
125½Mission Pool Hall

SAN FRANCISCO W—Cont'd
127 Kahn's Shoe Store
127½El Ortiz Barber Shop
129 Carpenters Hall
129½△Ry Ex Agcy
131△Dendahl's
Galisteo bg ss
200△Faith Cafe
201-3 Candelario's Indian Trading Post
203△Four Roses Beer Garden
204-8△Livingston H & Co
205 Giles J W Saddlery
205½Santa Fe Tailoring Co
207△City Cash Mkt
Burro al bg ns
209△Lensic Sandwich Shop
210△Maytag Shop
Pond's Elec Co
211△Lensic Theatre
Salmon Nathan
Greer Loan Co
Salmon & Green Inc
212△Coney Island
213 Vacant
214△Duran's Shoe Shop
215 **Lensic Theatre Building**
△Smith W H
Lensic Club
△Berardinelli M V
△Federal Housing Admn
216 Q & O Cafe
217 Vacant
218△Mac's Feed Store
219△Lensic Tavern
220 Albuq Nat Gas Co whose
221△Albuq Natural Gas Co
222-24△Santa Fe Hay & Grain
Co
Fidel Bros
223 Lensic Barber Shop
223½Carroll D S
225△Muralter's Clnrs & Tailors
225½Vacant
226△Duran Pablo
Silva Frank
228 Santa Cruz Valley
Pro Co
229△Silver Dollar Bar
230 Eagle Bar
231△Burleson Bros Clnrs
232 Eagle Cafe & Rooms
233△Park Lndry
Sandoval bg ss
301 Quintana B & Co
304 Vacant
305△Muller's Garage
Santa Fe-Chama Valley
Transp Co
Heren S E
306(1) Ross J W
306(2-3) Vacant
306(4)△Waddell Norman
308 Cash Price Frame Shop

309△Big Jo Lumber Co
312 Lopez Luis
313½Big Jo Lbr Co whse
314-14½Vacant
316-18 Ortiz Beatriz ⓒ
319-21 **Devendorf Apts**
Apartments—
*1△Devendorf C W ⓒ
*2 Guziel A A
*3 Prescott J D
*4 Julien T E
*5 Fegan A F
*6 Taylor J R
*7 Daugherty D M
*8△Vreeland Grace
*9 Kahre Alfred
*10 Murphy M A Mrs
*11 Edwards H E
Street Continued
320 Eddy Margarita Mrs
322 Armijo Albert
322½Iaragouni James
324 Baca Lola Mrs ⓒ
324½Kelley Loraine
327 Bohos Thos
328 Crook T S
331 Ethelbah Mary Mrs
Jefferson intersects
402 Vacant
403-5 Huffaker V J
404 Vacant
406△Paul E R ⓒ
407 Valdez Elias
408 Vacant
411 Armijo A R
412 Casados Victor ⓒ
415-17△McCrosson Hand
Woven Textiles
421 Erwin M T Mrs ⓒ
422 Maes Max
422½Vacant
423 Vacant
425 Chavez Juan ⓒ
425½Gonzalez Maria ⓒ
427 Vacant
428 Jacinto Zenobia
429 Guillen Rose Mrs
430 Garcia Catarina
433△Martinez A B
rear Ortiz Canuto
434 Donahue J M
437 Montoya Ursula
438 Conklin Refugio Miss ⓒ
439 Padilla E M Mrs
439½Vacant
441 Ortiz Damian
443△Gomez J B
rear Cruz Miguel
446 Mascarell L D Mrs ⓒ
447 Vacant
Park av bg ss
450 El Pueblito Gro
511 Duran Evaristo ⓒ
515 Vacant

Figure 45. Page from Hudspeth's 1940 Santa Fe City Directory, showing the businesses on West San Francisco Street.

SAN ANTONIO—(Cont'd)
501△Gilbert Carlos ◎
511△Ortiz Arthur ◎
554△Clauser D M ◎
555△May I N
558△Hauskins Eunice Mrs
627 Vacant
630 Alire Juanita Mrs
rear Alire Abelino
632 Allen Gwendoline Mrs

SANCHEZ
Begins 539 College ext east (Right Even)
307 Pacheco H G ◎
309 Ortiz M G ◎
310 Valencia Manuela ◎
325 Martinez J M ◎
327 Salazar Joaquin ◎
329 Moulton Alice Mrs

SANDOVAL
Begins 300 W San Francisco ext south (Right Even)
102-4 Vacant
104½△Waddell Cabt Shop
106△Gardner Elec Co
106½ Vacant
108 Fixit Shop
109 Clark Irene
110 Cruz Antonio
111 Moya Fred
112 Pictorial Signs Shop
113 Peterson Allene Mrs
114 Martinez M C shoemkr
115 La Febre T J
116-18 Vacant
117 Valdez Benigno
119 Maestas Florence Mrs
121△Gomez David
123 Tamaulipas Cafe
W Water intersects

SAN FRANCISCO EAST
South side of Plaza begins at Don Gaspar av ext east (Right Odd)
50-52△Penney J C Co dry gds
54△Kaune Gro Co
54½ **Spitz Building**
△Wright E R lawyer
Immanuel Luth Ch
△Hoover D N lawyer
56△Zook Pharmacy
58-62△Woolworth F W Co dept store
62½△Goodman Men's Store
64△Mayflower Cafe Cocktail Rm
66△Mayflower Cafe
68△Plaza Hotel
△Postal Tel-Cable Co
70△Santa Fe Jewel Shop
72△Recreation Club
74△Moore's clo
76△Masonic Temple
76½△Spitz Jewelry Store & Gift Shop
78 **Gans Building**
Rooms—
*3△Errett H H real est
*6-7△Wolfe E F dentist
*8△Broaddus W H optometrist
*10△Patterson W S oil opr
Warn F R oil opr
*11△Amer Natl Ins Co
*12△Barker C B lawyer
*14△Richards J J real est
*15△Harvey J C eng
*17△Amer Loan Corp
Street Continued
80△Southwest Arts & Crafts
82△Capital Pharmacy
Contl Air Lines
T W A
84△Stromberg's Men's Wear
Shelby intersects
100△La Fonda hotel
Harvey Fred Inc
La Fonda News Stand
La Fonda Indian Shop
La Fonda Barber Shop
La Fonda Beauty Shop
101-3△A T & S F Ry
105△Tohill N M optometrist
107△Dorman H H ins
109△Camera Shop
Stevenson P H ins
Native Prod Co
Hendrix Engr Serv
111△Fiske E W phys
111½△Seth & Montgomery lawyers
115△Spanish & Ind Trad Co
115½ New Mexico State Record
122△St Francis Paroch Sch
123△Postoffice
Cathedral pl intersects

SAN FRANCISCO WEST
South side of Plaza begins at Don Gaspar av ext west and divides intersecting streets into north and south (Right Odd)
100-2△Santa Fe Book & S Co
104½ **Laughlin Building**
Rooms—
*3-4△Mera F E phys
*6△City Fin Co
*7-8△Claffey F J dentist
*9-12△Bowman H S lawyer
Mell J D lawyer
*15△Clancy A H lawyer
*16-17△Glenn J F dentist
*22-23△Barton W C phys
*24-28△Barker & McGinnis lawyers
*26△Associated Contr of N M

SAN FRANCISCO W—(Ct'd)
*27△Neel Geo M eng
Street Continued
105△Nancy's clo
105½ **Renehan Building**
Rooms—
*1-2△Brooks Ed ins
Calvin J F real est
Espe Ins Agcy
*3△Central Typewriter Agcy
*4△W P A
*8△Capital City Coml Coll
*300△Heath W L chiro
*316△N Y Life Ins Co
*317-20△Gilbert & Hamilton lawyers
*321△Staplin Frank oil opr
Street Continued
106△Yontz H C Jewelry Store
106½ Pflueger's shoes
107-9△Butt's Central Pharm
108 Clarke J F
109½ **Salmon Building**
Rooms—
*1-2△McIntosh C R lawyer
*3-4△Holloman Reed lawyer
Harris Delia L sten
*5-7△Kiker & Sanchez lawyers
Albert A J lawyer
*14-15△Gutierrez M P lawyer
Thomas Eva lawyer
*18△Montoya J M lawyer
*19△Democratic State Hdqtrs
*20-22△Lujan Manuel Agcy ins
Old Line Mutual Ben Assn
*24 McCaskill Scoville
*29△N M Liquor Dealers Assn
*30 Abeyta Alex
*32 Garcia Clara
*34 Sandoval Benj
Street Continued
110△Ballard's gro
111△Emporium dry gds
112△Taichert's Variety Store
113△O K Barber Shop
O K Beauty Shop
114△Pay Less Drug Store
Louis Flower Shop
115△Santa Fe Clo Store
117△Calif Store clo
118△Bell's Dept Store
118½ **Galisteo Building**
N M Dept Pub Welfare
119△Bank Bar
120△Kahn's Shoe Store
121 Paris Pop Corn & Candy Shop
121½ Dominguez Adolfo
122△Beer's Ready-to-Wear
123△Paris Theatre
123½ Paris Shoe Shine Parlor
125△New Canton Cafe
125½ Cactus Shop curios
127△Cartwright Hdw Co
127½ Santa Fe Candy Kitchen
129 **Don Juan Bldg**
△Santa Fe Sec Sch
△Mutual Life Ins Co
Galisteo bg ss
129½△Ry Exp Agcy
131△Dendahl's dry gds
200△Faith Cafe
201-3 Candelario's Indian Trading Post
203△Billia's Frank Bar
204-8△Livingston H & Co furn
205 Vacant
205½△Santa Fe Tailoring Co
207△City Cash Mkt
Burro al bg ns
209△Lensic Sandwich Shop
210△Burro Alley Theatre
209-15 **Lensic Theatre Bldg**
△Lensic Theatre
△Salmon Nathan
△Greer Loan Co
△Salmon & Greer real est
△Smith W H chiro
△Bernardelli M V dentist
△N M Highway Planning Survey
210 Santa Fe Loan Co
Ortiz G A jwlr
212△Mode O'Day clo
213 Vacant
214△Griffin Elec Co
216 Chili King Cafe
217△Santa Fe Press
218△Dependable Gro & Mkt
219△Lensic Night Club
220 Coronado Barber Shop
221△Mission Pool Hall
222-24 Vacant
223 Lensic Barber Shop
223½ Allen Angel C
224½ Santa Fe Meat Mkt
225△Muralter's Clnrs
226△Duran Pablo real est
228 Rios Tiburcio curios
228a Eagle Bar
228½ Reno Rooms
229△Silver Dollar Bar
230 Reno Cafe
231 Casino Cafe
233 Vacant
Sandoval bg ss
301 Capitol City Bicycle Co
305△Mullen's Serv Sta
306 **Apartments**
*1△Waddell N O
*2 Hassell S W
*3 Hutcheson E L Mrs
308△W P A
309-15△Big Jo Lumber Co
312 La Barca restr
314 Kelly A E Mrs
314½ Gallegos Ezequiel
316-18 Perez Ignacio restr
310-25 **Devendorf Apts**

Figure 46. Advertisement showing Louis' Flower Shop (center) in Pay Less Drug Store. *Santa Fe New Mexican*, Jan. 19, 1940.

121 West San Francisco Street, which is further down the street (west) on your right (north), was the site of the Paris Pop Corn and Candy Shop, owned and operated by James (John) G. Zervas (Figs. 47, 48). Zervas was born in 1885, immigrated in 1909, and was naturalized by 1930. He appeared in the 1930 and 1950 U.S. Censuses as living in Santa Fe. In the 1930 Census he was a cook at a cafe. He did not appear in the Santa Fe City Directories of 1930-1934, but in 1936 he was listed as pantry man at La Fonda Hotel, which was also listed as his residence. By 1938 he was listed as proprietor of the Paris Pop Corn and Candy Shop and was apparently living in the back of the shop. By 1942 he moved his residence into an apartment above the shop at 121 ½ West San Francisco Street. His listings continued in the 1944 City Directory. In the 1947 City Directory, both Zervas and the Paris Pop Corn and Candy Shop were both gone. 121 West San Francisco Street was now vacant, and 121 ½ was not listed at all. Zervas never again appeared in a Santa Fe City Directory. He did however appear in the 1950 U.S. Census, working at Dora Nusbaum's apartments at 121-123 Washington Avenue. He might have been working in linen supply and laundry, as these words were written and then crossed out by the census taker. Zervas was 65 at the time.

In 1946, at his shop Zervas sold "the famous" James Pappas' popcorn and hot dogs (Fig. 49). Pappas was a cook, first at Mutt & Jeff's on Galisteo Street in 1934, and then at La Bajada Café on Cerrillos Rd. in 1940.

That was between 1938 and 1947 or so. Later, by 1949, this site at 121 West San Francisco Street became the second Mitchell's Music and Appliance Store. The first Mitchell's Music Store was established two years earlier in 1947 down the street at 205 West San Francisco Street. So, in 1949, Mitchell turned the first music store at 205 into Mitchell's (Army) Surplus Store and opened the second music store up the street at 121. Those of us who are Old Timers remember these businesses well !

123 West San Francisco Street next door was the site of the Paris Theatre. On Saturdays, the Paris would have special movies for kids, without news reels as we were at war. I remember watching The Lone Ranger, Tarzan, Bud Abbot and Lou Costello Meet Frankenstein, and other favorites of the time. Google an excerpt on YouTube and let yourself become a ten-year old at the Paris! While you're at it, I'll take a popcorn please!

M E N U

FIESTA SPECIAL

2 Dishes for 2 Monsters

SPAGHETTI ala Mussolini and SAUER KRAUT ala Hitler

FRIED in

G R E E C E

PARIS POP CORN and CANDY SHOP

Santa Fe, N. M.

JAMES ZERVAS

Figure 47. Advertisement for the Paris Popcorn and Candy Shop. *Santa Fe New Mexican*, August 29, 1940.

Figure 48. Advertisement from the *Santa Fe New Mexican*, Feb. 10, 1942. Three of these advertised businesses were Greek-owned and operated and are discussed in this book.

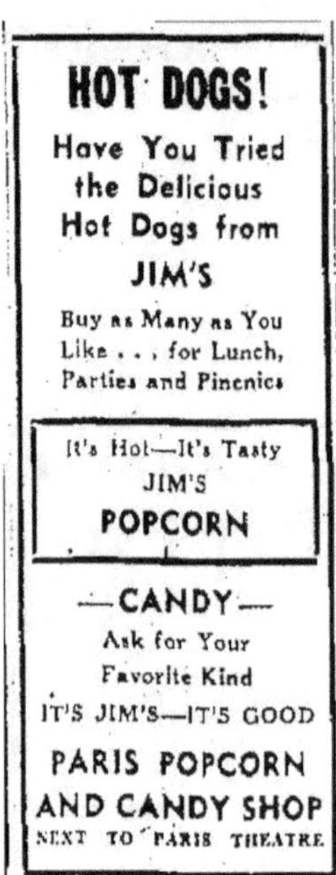

Figure 49. Advertisement for the Paris Popcorn and Candy Shop. *Santa Fe New Mexican*, Feb. 9, 1946.

On the same side of the street and a few doors down at 127½ West San Francisco Street was the site of Dennis Market's Santa Fe Candy Kitchen (Fig. 50). Market (wife Evelyn) was born in 1895 in Greece and immigrated in 1910 to Wisconsin, where he attended night school and took an apprenticeship as a confectioner. He enlisted with the U.S. Armed Forces, served with the 1st Infantry Division in WWI and was wounded. In 1936, he and his wife moved to Santa Fe during the Great Depression "to make a new start." The Santa Fe Candy Kitchen appeared for the first time in the 1938 Santa Fe City Directory. Market and his wife struggled and eventually developed a candy using Pinon nuts that they bought exclusively from Native Americans who transported them into Santa Fe on burros. The store also sold a wide selection of newspapers, magazines, and comic books. Market passed at age 66 in 1961 but his wife continued the business at least through 1965. He was a member of the American Legion and Masonic Lodge.

From 1949 to 1950, Market took George Chilimidos (wife Arretta, a nurse from Missouri) as partner.

Figure 50. Advertisement for the Santa Fe Candy Kitchen. *Santa Fe New Mexican*, May 16, 1939.

We now walk westward past the intersection of West San Francisco Street and Galisteo Street, where we enter the 200 block of West San Francisco Street.

On your left or the south side of the street is 200 West San Francisco Street. From 1934 this was the site of the Faith Café (Figs. 51, 52). As a corner site it had two addresses: 200 West San Francisco Street, and 106 Galisteo Street. There were no such addresses in 1928. Instead, 202-208 West San Francisco Street, and 106 Galisteo Street, were occupied by Livingstone H. & Co., a furniture store. By 1936, in addition to the Faith Café at 200 West San Francisco Street, Green Import Stores was listed at 204-206 (there was no 202), and Livingstone was listed at 208. By 1940, Livingstone occupied 204-208.

The Faith Café was opened in June 1934 by Paul Kellis and Steve Anthony. In 1936, Kellis had left for Gallup and it was now owned by Steve Anthony (wife Lillie) and Alex Kalanges (Kalangis), wife Efterpi or Ethel.

Paul Kellis was born in 1902 in Turkey. He did not appear in the 1930 U.S. Census. As discussed, he was in Santa Fe from at least 1934 to 1936 but did not appear in any Santa Fe City Directory. Later, in the 1940 U.S. Census, he was listed as living in Los Angeles. In 1942 he registered for the draft, with Steve Karman in Gallup as his contact. In the 1950 U.S. Census, he was listed as living in Gallup. He passed in 1970 and was buried in Albuquerque.

Steve Anthony was born in 1896 or 1897 in Greece. He was married to Lillie from at least 1934 to 1944. His biography was previously discussed in Chapter 2 on Lincoln Avenue and the Plaza Café.

Alex or Alecco (wife Efterpi or Ethel) Kalanges (Kalangis) (Fig. 53) was born in Smyrna, Turkey in 1899. Alex immigrated in 1915 and first went to Manistique, Michigan, where he had a cousin. In 1934 he returned to Greece and married Efterpi or Ethel, born 1913. They returned to Manistique. Efterpi felt it was too cold so in 1935 they moved to Santa Fe, where she had a cousin, Steve Anthony, and an uncle, Gus Kalavantes (Kalavantis). By 1944, Steve and Lillie Anthony divorced and Steve sold the restaurant to Alex Kalanges. Alex and Efterpi had two children, Cornelia and Sarando or Ike. Alex passed away in 1954. Alex was remembered as a great and caring father. He was an active member of AHEPA, the Greek Orthodox Church, and the Elks. His wife Efterpi and their two children ran the cafe after Alex passed. Efterpi passed in 2002.

Figure 51. Interior of the Faith Café. Photo courtesy of the Kalangis family.

Figure 52.
Advertisement for the reopening of the Faith Café.
Santa Fe New Mexican, June 8, 1934.

Figure 53. Kalangis family. Sarando, Efterpi, Alecco, and Cornelia.
Photo courtesy of the Kalangis family.

Nicolas or Nick K. Falaris was a cashier and waiter at the Faith Café probably starting after WWII, and was a floater for all Greek restaurants. He was known as Kokala (bones) because he was very skinny. He was born in either 1897 or 1901. He first appeared in Santa Fe in 1942 as a cook at the Burro Alley Café at 201 West San Francisco Street. He enlisted and served with the U.S. Armed Forces in WWII. He lived with the Kartas family of the Savoy Café. He passed away in 1982.

Nicholas Haralambus Gallanos (Galanos, aka Wouthis) was a cook at the Faith Café in 1952. He was born in Turkey in 1905 and immigrated in 1919. In 1934 he was in Santa Fe, married to Lola, and working as a cook. In 1938 he was a waiter at the Plaza Café. He was now married to Bernadita and was petitioning for naturalization. Apparently he had divorced Lola and married Bernadita, who had three children. In 1940 and 1942 he was a cook at a location undetermined but his name appears in a 1940 advertisement in the *Santa Fe New Mexican* for Butts Central Pharmacy listing "personnel of our friendly store." In 1947 he was a cook at the Plaza Café. In 1958 his wife was a waitress at the El Fidel Coffee Shop on Galisteo Street and in 1960 Nicholas was a manager there. In 1965 he appeared in an advertisement in the *Santa Fe New Mexican* for De Vargas Coffee Shop at the De Vargas Hotel, stating the coffee shop was now under his management. He was a veteran of the Merchant Marines, spoke seven languages, and was conversant in Middle East affairs. He passed away in 1979 and was buried in Rosario Cemetery.

Nick Maryol worked at the Faith Café for his relative Efterpi Kalangis who also came from the village of Kalloni on the island of Lesbos.

Gus Volos (Valos, Valus) was a manager at the Faith Café from at least 1950 to 1955, after which he moved to the El Fidel Coffee Shop on Galisteo Street to at least 1959. Volos was born in 1891 in Greece.

Across the street from the Faith Café (200 West San Francisco Street) was 201-203 West San Francisco Street, the site of Candelario's Indian Trading Post. 203 West San Francisco Street at the same time was Frank Billia's Bar, so the businesses were somehow sharing addresses.

203 West San Francisco Street in 1946 was purchased by Pete C. Dakis (Hadzidakis) and reopened as La Mariposa Bar. Later in 1953, Pete owned a liquor store in Cuyamungue. Pete registered for the draft in Dawson, Colfax County in 1917, so he was likely a miner. In 1929 he was a waiter at the Court Café in Albuquerque. In 1931 he was in Denver, in the soft drinks business. In 1940 he was arrested in Santa Fe for gambling. In 1942 he appeared in Santa Fe City Directory as Pete Dakos, and was administrator of the estate of Jim Sitsas. In 1947 he appeared in the Santa Fe City Directory as owner of La Mariposa. He was born in 1891 and passed in 1983.

Next door, 205 West San Francisco Street in 1942 was the site of Tom's Music & Furniture, Thomas Langas (Longas), proprietor. Langas started out on 222 Galisteo Street with his store Tom the Hatter, which is later discussed in Chapter 6.

In 1944 it was Tom's Music Store.

In 1947 it was Mitchell's Music Store, Gus Mitchell, proprietor.

In 1949 it was Mitchell's (Army) Surplus Store.

Continuing on the north side of the West San Francisco Street, we reach the Lensic Theatre Building with addresses 209-215 (odd numbers).

209 West San Francisco Street was the site of the Lensic Sandwich Shop. It was owned by Harry Dakos (wife Bernice) (Fig. 54) and Pete Theodore (Fig. 55) in 1934; by Pete Theodore from 1936 to 1938; and in 1940 by Paul Pagis. In 1934, Harry Dakos' wife Bernice was a waitress at the Santa Fe Chocolate Shop and their son James was a clerk at the Sandwich Shop.

James Karamouzis was listed as a waiter in 1936.

Pete Columbus (wife Toula) was listed as a cook in 1940.

In 1942 the Lensic Sandwich Shop was replaced by the Santa Fe Creamery #2 which was not owned by Greeks.

Figure 54. Inside the Pomonis residence. Frolm left to right: Louis Carrelas, Harry Dakos (with left arm raised). The women with flowers in their hair were Efterpi Kalangis (left) and Fannie Assimakis (right). The women on the far right with her back to the camera was Alexandra Kartas. Jan. 25, 1945 at Tom Pomonis' Name Day (see Figure 27). Photo from author's collection.

Figure 55. Inside the Mayflower Cocktail Lounge, c. 1940. Left to right: Pete Theodore, unknown, Mike Kartas, unknown, Harry Dakos. Photo from author's collection.

John Mastoras, or Johnnie, was listed as candymaker at the Lensic Sandwich Shop in 1936 and as cook in 1938 and he lived at the Plaza Hotel. Johnnie previously owned the New Mexico Candy Kitchen at 204 West Central Avenue in Albuquerque before he moved to Santa Fe to work at the Lensic Sandwich Shop. Johnnie appeared in the 1920 U.S. Census in Albuquerque as a helper in a confectionary, sharing a room with another Greek man, Sheer Mitchell, at 222 East Grand Avenue. Johnnie passed away in 1939 after only three years in Santa Fe and was buried locally at Fairview Cemetery. He had been a member of the American Hellenic Education Progressive Association, or AHEPA, and they took charge of the burial services. His funeral notice states that people liked Johnnie because Johnnie liked people, that children would wait for him to take their candy orders because he would always give them a little extra. Nearly ninety years after his passing, people were still decorating his grave at Christmas.

John Mastoras' burial plot is located next to that of John Torakis and Andrew P. Anitsakis (Fig. 56). John Torakis' brother, Mike Torakis, was one of the pallbearers at Mastoras' funeral; as was Andy Anitsakis, who had worked with John Torakis as a miner in Colfax County in 1930, and who would be buried adjacent the two later in 1954. Other Santa Fe restaurateurs also served as pallbearers, namely Steve Kutrulis chef of the KC Waffle House, John Caravanas of the Coney Island Café and the Burro Alley Café, and Gus Koulas of the Liberty Café.

Figure 56. Grave markers for Andrew Anitsakis, John Torakis, and John Mastoras, at the Santa Fe Fairview Cemetery. Photograph by Yorgos Marinakis.

210 West San Francisco Street across on the south side of the street was not occupied by Greeks prior to 1940. But in 1940 it became the site of the Burro Alley Café, John Karvanos proprietor. Nicolas or Nick K. Falaris was a cook there in 1942.

By 1944 it was the Burro Alley Liquor Store.

By 1947 it was the Burro Alley Café and Liquor Store and it was owned by John Komis. By 1958 he changed the name to El Patio Café & Bar. Komis had returned from the war and was living at the Plaza Hotel. Komis was born in 1914 on the Greek island of Cephalonia. He married Lemonia and had a son Nick. He passed in 1994.

210 West San Francisco Street was also contemporaneously the site of the Burro Alley Theatre owned by Salmon & Greer. Nathan Greer also owned the Lensic Theatre across the street. By 1949 there was no longer a Burro Alley Liquor Store or Theatre but the Lensic Theatre still stands as of this printing. The Burro Alley Café became Tia Sophia's Restaurant in 1975. It is owned by a son of Georgia Maryol, who was proprietor of the Mayflower on Water Street from 1964 to 1973. Georgia is now proprietor of Tomasita's.

212 West San Francisco Street, still on the south side of the street and opposite the Lensic Theater, was the site of the Coney Island Café. It was run in 1932 by Michael Kartas and John Kirvanis (Karvanos), in 1934 by Kirvanis, 1936 by Kirvanis and Steve Coronas, and 1938 by Kirvanis. By 1940 the address was occupied by Mode O'Day, a clothing store. The cafe at one point employed Steve Kutulas, who does not appear in the City Directory.

In 1940, Andy Anitsakis was a cook at the Chili King Café and in 1947 he was a cook at the Coney Island Café. He later worked as a clerk at the Cerrillos Liquor Store, where he was shot and killed during a robbery in 1954. Andy had been robbed there at gunpoint twice. Proprietor Tom Pomonis had told him, if you are robbed, just give them the money. Thomas M. Moore was identified as the suspect while he was in custody for a federal crime, because one of the guns he had in his possession when he was arrested was found to belong to Anitsakis. Moore confessed, saying he never intended to shoot, but Anitsakis ducked into the back room and came out shooting to kill. Moore shot him and took his gun. He received a sentence of 99 years, of which he likely at most served 15 years.

Anitsakis was born in 1895 in Chania, Crete, and immigrated in 1909. Anitsakis appeared in the 1930 U.S. Census in Colfax County, working as a miner with several other Greeks from Chania, including John Torakis, who was born in 1893 and who immigrated in 1906. These men were in their 40's and were still mining. John Torakis registered for the WWI draft in 1918 while working in Koehler, Colfax County as a miner. John Torakis passed in 1938.

John Torakis' brother Emmanuel Georgiou Torakis, or Mike Torakis, immigrated in 1907, worked as a landlord and petitioned for citizenship in 1945. Mike Torakis worked in the mines of Trinidad before moving to Santa Fe where he had a career managing real estate. Mike had a dog named Tito and "lived as a hermit" off Montezuma Avenue. There were newspapers on his floor and he loved chocolate and a shot of whiskey. In the 1950 U.S. Census he was listed as sharing a house at 223 ½ Montezuma (at Montezuma and Galisteo) with Guss Themas and working as a camp ground manager (There was a Camp Fort Marcy tourist camp at 755 Cerrillos Road.). Ike Kalanagis related how Mike asked if he could fly with him to Crete so he could die there. When Ike picked up Mike at his house, Mike had all of his worldly belongings packed into two paper grocery sacks and they traveled that way to Greece. We don't know when his dog Tito passed. Mike Torakis passed away in 1973 in Greece. Mike Torakis paid for the grave plots at Fairview Cemetery for both John Torakis and for Andrew Anitsakis (Fig. 56).

213 West San Franciso Street in the Lensic Building, in 1942 was the site of the Lensic Dispensary, a liquor store, owned and operated by Evangelo Asterio.

214 West San Francisco Street, across the street, in 1944, was the site of the Burro Alley Cigar Store owned and operated by Mary Pappas. Pappas was previously a waitress at the De Vargas Café, from 1936 to 1938. She was a widow, born in Colorado, so we do not know if she had her name by ethnicity or by marriage. Her business was nestled alongside and across the street from other Greek businesses. She did not appear in the 1940 or 1942 City Directories but she appeared in the 1940 U.S. Census as a restaurant owner. Steve "Papas," a miner, and his wife Mary, appeared in the 1934 Santa Fe City Directory, but in the 1930 U.S. Census they were living Colfax County, and Mary "Papas" was about 12 years younger than Mary Pappas and was born in New Mexico rather than Colorado. So, they were likely two different women.

216 West San Francisco Street next door was the site of the Chili King Café, owned by John Hagidakis (Hagis) in 1940, and George Tsintsiras from 1942 to at least 1960. Hagidakis passed in 1940. He had two cousins in Santa Fe: Pete Dakis, and Antonio Andreakis who served as administrator

of his estate. Hagidakis had been a miner in Colfax County before coming to Santa Fe.

George K. Tsintsiras was born in 1901 in Scortsinou, Greece. In 1938 he was a helper at the Laguna Café on Galisteo Street. In 1940 he owned a cafe in Albuquerque. After John Hagidakis passed in 1940, Tsintsiras bought the Chili King Café. Tsintsiras lived for many years at the Montezuma Hotel. He registered for the U.S. WWII draft in 1942 in Santa Fe. He never married and passed in 1978.

If you were to continue walking west, you would reach Sandoval Street and then North Guadalupe Street. But we are not continuing west because this is the last address on our tour on West San Francisco Street. Please turn around and backtrack to the intersection of Galisteo Street.

GALISTEO

6
GALISTEO STREET

We begin this part of the walking tour at the intersection of West San Francisco Street and Galisteo Street. This next part of our walking tour takes us south down Galisteo Street towards the Santa Fe River (Map 5, Fig. 57). Galisteo Street at the time was home to a liquor store, bars, a pool hall, and hotels, but the Governor's Mansion was also just down the block.

The 100 block of Galisteo runs from West San Francisco Street to Water Street The 200 block of Galisteo runs from Water Street to Alameda and the Santa Fe River. The 300 block of Galisteo runs from West De Vargas to Montezuma. Even numbered addresses are on your right (west), odd numbered addresses on your left (east).

The address we begin with, at the corner of West San Francisco Street and Galisteo Street, is 106 Galisteo Street. It was also listed as 200 West San Francisco Street as it was located on the corner of the two streets. It was occupied by the Faith Café, discussed in the previous chapter.

Further south down Galisteo Street is 108 Galisteo Street, occupied by the Capital Liquor Store. It was owned and operated in 1944 by Louis Paulos. Paulos was born in 1897 in Greece. Between 1940 and 1944 he worked as a salesman for the Charles Ilfeld Company and lived at the El Fidel Hotel. By the 1950 U.S. Census he was listed as unable to work and passed away that year.

The next two entries are provided as landmarks for your walking tour. They were not Greek-owned businesses.

On your right, 110-112 Galisteo Street was occupied by the Blue Ribbon Canteen, better known as the infamous "George King's Bar"! It was a loud and rowdy bar, and women would cross the street to avoid being whistled at!

120-124 Galisteo Street, at the northwest corner of Galisteo Street and Water Street, was occupied by the El Cid restaurant (120) and bar (124).

We then cross Water Street into the 200 block of Galisteo Street. At the southwest corner of Galisteo Street and Water Street, 202-204 Galisteo Street was occupied by the Hotel El Fidel, owned and operated by the Fidel Brothers. There were several businesses in the El Fidel Hotel Building that were owned or operated by Greeks.

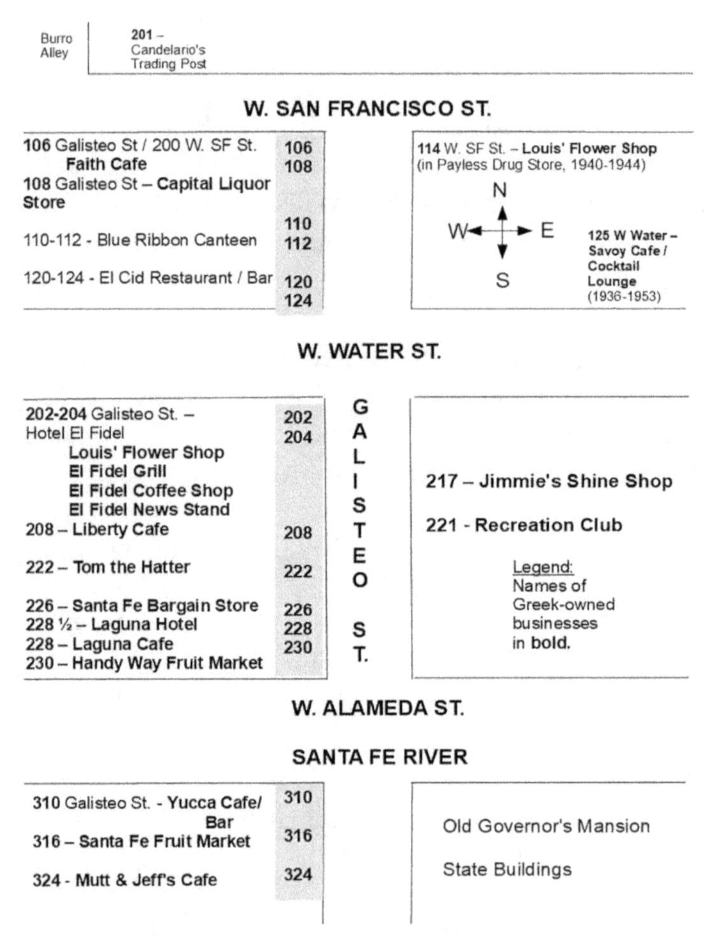

Map 5. Galisteo Street. North is at the top of the page.

SANTA FE BUILDERS SUPPLY COMPANY
EVERYTHING FOR THE BUILDER
Office-Yard, Foot Montezuma Ave.
PHONE 100

FRANKLIN AV
Begins 631 Agua Fria extends south 2 blks to Hickox
518 Lyckman A W
520 Smith R E
521 Chavez M C
524 Blea Eulalio
527 Davy H C
528 Gutierrez Juan
530 Rael Abenicio
535 Gutierrez Lorenzo
536 Sanchez Amalia
537 Gilcrease Felix
540 Howell Harry
542 Jackson W C
543 Vacant
544 Prevost Floyd
545 Thora Mack
546 Bietsch C W
547 Smith F W
548 Hagman C B
550 Loucks J A
Hickox intersects
609 Smith W F
611 Vacant
619 Lopez G G
621 Thomas R F
622 Pino Juan
625 Pankey R W
626 Rivera Luis
627 Trujillo Patrick

GALISTEO
Begins 200 W San Francisco extends south beyond city limits
106 Faith Cafe
107 N M State Emp Serv
108 Harper Dress Shoppe
110-12 Blue Ribbon Canteen
116 La Fonda Barber Shop
Ortiz G A
118 Economy Shoe Shop
120-24 El Cid Campeador
W Water intersects
cor Magnolia Pet Co
Ragle Paul Serv Sta
Paul's U-Drive It Car Co
202-4 Hotel El Fidel
El Fidel Cigar and News Stand
El Fidel Grill
206 State Highway Dept
208 El Fidel Beauty Serv
210 Paris Shoe Store
211 Nine Eight Taxi
212-14 Roybal Theo Store
215-17 Quality Press
219 Santa Fe Cycle Shop
220-22 Olivas Juan
223 Lac Signs Shop
224 Silver Star Shoe Shop
Combination Cafe
225 Vacant
226 Alameda Bar
227-31 Sinclair Ref Co
228 Laguna Cafe
228½ Politis Wm
232 Safeway Stores
Rio Santa Fe intersects
W De Vargas intersects
302 Kiesov's
308 Sanitary Steam Bakery
310 Gutierrez J V
312 Sanitary Gro & Mkt
314-16 Santa Fe Fruit Mkt
318-20 Brock Uphol & Matt Shop
322 Spike's Clnr Hatters & Dyers
324 Mutt & Jeff Cafe
326 S S S Mess Serv
nw cor Santa Fe Motor Co used car lot
Montezuma intersects
sw cor Phillips Pet Co
N Capitol ends es
es Capitol bldg
408 N M Public Welfare Bldg
W P A
U S Treas Dept Disb Office
424 Alarid H C
426 Martinez Victoriano
432 Valdez Alfredo
S Capitol ends es
Cerrillos rd bg ws
435 Vacant
439 Alarid Amadeo
440 Pflueger Jno
443 McKenzie Donald
449 Romero Ramon
rear Romero Ramon Jr
454 Gerdes G P Mrs
W Manhattan intersects
504 Hosack W J
rear Hensley A B Mrs
506 Romero Bernabe
510 Henry Viola Mrs
514 Rivera Juan
518 Vacant
521 Sargent D H Mrs
530 Braner R J
Hickox bg ws
Santa Fe av bg es
600 Ortiz F S
601 Vacant
604 LeBou Lottie Mrs
rear LeBou T E
605 Garcia Romulo
rear Garcia Casimiro
607 Martinez Irineo
609 Garcia C H Mrs
rear Martinez Armando
610 Romero Casimiro
612 Casados Magdaleno
rear Martinez Bernabe

Building Material
Cement
Glass
Heating Equipment
Stoves and Ranges
Lime
Lumber
Electric Supplies
Paints
Hardware
Plumbing Supplies
Pumps
Windmills
Roofing Material
Sash and Doors
Varnishes
Wallboard

Figure 57. Page from Hudspeth's 1936 Santa Fe City Directory showing the businesses on Galisteo Street.

From 1936–1937, William Assimakis was proprietor of the El Fidel Grill. In 1938, Pete (wife Matilda) Kopanos worked there as a cook.

In 1944, as mentioned in the previous chapter, Louis' Flower Shop, Louis Peppers (Pepperis) proprietor, moved from 141 West San Francisco Street in the Pay Less Drug Store to the El Fidel Hotel on Galisteo Street. We don't know for sure where he came from. There was a Louis Peppers from Greece in the 1930 U.S. Census living in Ponca City, Oklahoma, age 40, with Guss Peppers, age 43, where both were cooks in cafes. Later, in 1958, Louis Pepperis was reported in the Santa Fe newspaper as being admitted to a Santa Fe hospital. There we lose track of him. There is a grave for Louis J. Peppers in River Grove, Cook County, Illinois, born 1886 and died 1981, but we don't know if this was the same man.

In 1945, John Samaris (Samalis) and Gus Kalavantes bought the El Fidel Coffee Shop (Fig. 58). Later that year, Kalavantes sold his share in the Coffee Shop to Samaris. Samaris operated it alone until at least 1947, when he was joined by Theodore (wife Vera) J. Peperas (Paperas, actually Papadomanolakis). The two men then bought the El Fidel News Stand from Fidel in 1951. In 1953, Peperas was the sole owner of the Coffee Shop and News Stand. But Peperas died in the same year, 1953, at age 60. Peperas was born in 1893 in Turkey and had four children with his wife Vera (Elvira Armijo, nee Rios) who was 30 years younger than him. Since Louis Peppers (Pepperis) moved his flower business into the El Fidel Hotel in 1944, and Theodore Peperas (Paperas) bought into a business in the El Fidel at least by 1947, it is possible that the Pepperis and Peperas men were cousins! There is a petition for naturalization by George Harry Papadomanolakis, dated 1942, and witnessed by Pete Theodore and Pete Dakis. George may have been a brother or cousin of Theodore Peperas.

Gus Kalavantes (Kalavantis), born in 1898 in Greece, was reported as having bought the El Fidel Coffee Shop, along with John Samalis (Samaris), in late April 1945 and reopening it on May 5, 1945 with seafood as their specialty (Fig. 58). Kalavantes was reported as having been a chef who cooked in many resorts around Los Angeles, which were known for their seafood. Five months later, Kalavantes sold his share to Samaris. He did not appear in either the 1944 or 1947 Santa Fe City Directories, nor in the 1930 or 1940 U.S. Censuses. He appeared in the 1950 U.S. Census, working in Gallup as a waiter. He is said to have returned to Greece. He was a cousin of Efterpi Kalangis of the Faith Café.

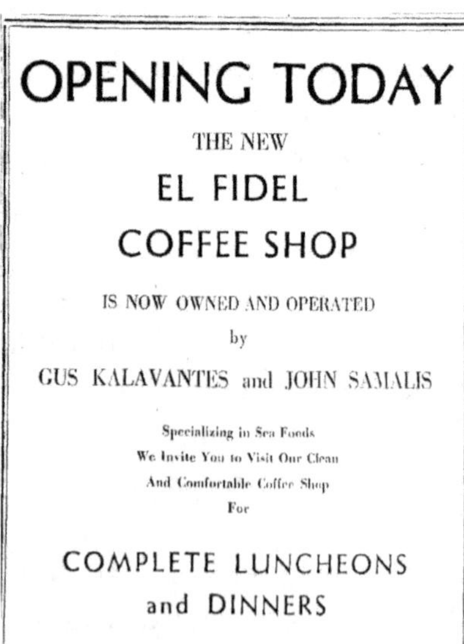

Figure 58. Advertisement for the New El Fidel Coffee Shop.
Santa Fe New Mexican, May 5, 1945.

Now we leave the El Fidel Building and continue south down Galisteo St, where, still on your right, we come to 208 Galisteo Street.

208 Galisteo Street was occupied by the Liberty Café (Fig. 59). It was opened in 1928 by Gus Koulas (wife Sophia from Poland) and Gust Razatos. The cafe operated through 1929. Gus Koulas was born in 1889 in Greece. Koulas had a Shoe Shine Parlor in Albuquerque at 209 ½ West Central prior to owning the Liberty Café in Santa Fe. By 1930, he was back in Albuquerque where he was proprietor of the Union Shining Parlor and later in 1935 he managed Selva's Dance Hall. Gus and Sophia Koulas had two children, Katherine (Kay) and William Gus Koulas (Gus Jr.). In 1942 Gus Jr. was working for the State and in that year he enlisted. In 1950 he was elected as a Democrat Justice of the Peace in White Rock. Gus (Sr.) passed in 1981 in Albuquerque.

Figure 59. Advertisement for the Liberty Café.
Santa Fe New Mexican, April 7, 1928.

Across the street at 217 Galisteo Street was Jimmie's Shine Shop, James Brogolos (Bragolis, Brogales), proprietor. Brogolos ran James Newstand from 1949 to 1950 at 320 Agua Fria. In 1951 he was a clerk at the Plaza Hotel. In 1953 he was a clerk at the El Fidel Hotel and married to Modesta, a dishwasher at the Plaza Café. In 1955 he opened his shoe shine shop on Galisteo. By 1958, Modesta was a widow.

Next door to Jimmie's was 221 Galisteo Street, occupied by the Recreation Club, a pool hall (Fig. 60). This pool hall moved from 72 East San Francisco Street to 221 Galisteo Street in 1946, as the Santa Fe Plaza was transitioning to tourist-focused businesses.

Figure 60. Advertisement for the Recreation Club.
Santa Fe New Mexican, April 16, 1946.

222 Galisteo Street across the street from the pool hall was occupied in 1938 by the store Tom the Hatter, Tom Langas (Longas), proprietor. Tom went on to open the Santa Fe Bargain Store in 1940 at 226 Galisteo Street, and then Tom's Music & Furniture in 1940 (renamed Tom's Music Store in 1942) at 205 West San Francisco. Langas lived next to his store at the Laguna Hotel. Langas was born in 1898 in Neohoriou, Tripolis, Greece. He immigrated in 1915 and petitioned for naturalization in 1924 (Fig. 61) when he was single and living in Caspar, Wyoming where there was a considerable mining industry. He passed in 1978.

ORIGINAL

No. 884

UNITED STATES OF AMERICA

DECLARATION OF INTENTION

State of Wyoming
County of Natrona } ss: In the District Court of Natrona County

I, Tom A. Langas, aged 27 years, occupation hat cleaner, do declare on oath that my personal description is: Color white; complexion dark; height 5 feet 6 inches; weight 138 pounds; color of hair black; color of eyes brown; other visible distinctive marks none

I was born in Neohorion, Tripolis, Greece on the 4th day of May, anno Domini 1898; I now reside at Kimball Romms, Casper, Wyo. I emigrated to the United States of America from Pereas, Greece on the vessel King Konstantine; my last foreign residence was Athens, Greece; I am not married; the name of my wife is ; she was born at and now resides at

It is my bona fide intention to renounce forever all allegiance and fidelity to any foreign prince, potentate, state, or sovereignty, and particularly to The Present Government of Greece of whom I am now a subject; I arrived at the port of New York in the State of N. Y., on or about the 15th day of September, anno Domini 1915; I am not an anarchist; I am not a polygamist nor a believer in the practice of polygamy; and it is my intention in good faith to become a citizen of the United States of America and to permanently reside therein: So help me God.

(Signed) TOM A. LANGAS

Subscribed and sworn to before me in the office of the Clerk of said Court this 31st day of December, anno Domini 1924

[SEAL OF COURT]

(Signed) Hazel Conwell Schilling

Clerk of the District Court.

(Signed) By Evelyn Ryan, Deputy Clerk.

(Photograph and signature of declarant named herein)

U. S. DEPARTMENT OF LABOR

BUREAU OF NATURALIZATION

This is to certify that the foregoing is a true copy of declaration of intention made by Tom A. Langas as shown by the records of the Bureau of Naturalization. This copy is invalid for all purposes after December 31, 1931, by reason of the expiration of seven years from the date the original declaration was made. This copy is issued under authority of Section 32 (a) of the act of June 29, 1906, as amended, and the seal of the Department of Labor hereunto affixed this 1st day of December, anno Domini 1931.

[SEAL]

Commissioner of Naturalization.

Application No. 18 B - 151

Form 2602

14—2014

Figure 61. Tom Longas' Petition for Naturalization.

We now continue south down Galisteo Street towards Alameda Street and the Santa Fe River.

228 Galisteo Street was occupied by the Laguna Café and 228 ½ Galisteo Street upstairs was occupied by the Laguna Hotel. From 1936 to 1940, the café was owned and operated by William Politis. In 1942, Politis added the hotel. By 1944, Politis sold the café to Louis Zagaris but kept ownership of the hotel. Politis was a member of the Permanent Committee of the 1941 Greek War Relief Association (Fig. 62; note his name on the notice), along with Louis D. Carellas, Pete Pomonis, Jim Ipiotis, Gus Mitchell, Pete Dakis, and Pete Theodore. Politis eventually opened the Laguna Bar in Alameda, a suburb of Albuquerque, which he sold in 1958. Politis passed in 1976.

In 1942, Steve (wife Reynalda) J. Coutroulis (Koutroulis, Kietrulis, Kutrulis) was cook at the Laguna Café & Hotel. Coutroulis was born in 1888 in Greece, registered for the draft in WWI while living in Colfax County where he probably worked in the mines, and passed in 1944. His wife Raynalda Alvord was born in Texas.

In 1936, Mike Keros was listed as a cook at the Laguna Café. Mike Kerrs (Keros) was born on the Greek island of Samos in 1884. He immigrated in 1904. According to his son Thee, Mike immigrated because his father was killed in a mill and he had to support his mother and four sisters and a brother. When Mike came to New York, he could not speak English so when he went into a restaurant, he would hear the word "hotcakes" and that is what he ate for a long time. Eventually he could speak English and Spanish. He appeared in the 1920 U.S. Census in Denver, Colorado, as a candy maker. He had a wife, Belva from Missouri, and two sons, Theofani (Thee, born 1913), and George (born 1917). We don't know why Mike went to Denver, but according to his son Thee, once he was there he learned candy making from Gust Razatos. (Gust moved to Santa Fe probably in 1920 and in 1923 Gust opened up the Santa Fe Chocolate Shop.) In 1927, Mike and Belva divorced in Colorado. Mike then appeared the next year in the 1928 Santa Fe City Directory. In the 1930 U.S. Census, Mike was now living and working in Durango as a candy maker, and his two sons Thee and George were living with their maternal uncle's family, Wood, in

Seibert, Colorado. By 1932, Mike was back again in Santa Fe at the Santa Fe Chocolate Shop. Mike passed away in 1953 at age 71.

In 1936, Mike Keros' son Thee Keros was listed in the Santa Fe City Directory as a bookkeeper at the First National Bank. In 1940, Thee Keros was married to Dorothy and was working at the First National Bank. They had two daughters, Barbara (6) and Katherine (4), suggesting they married in 1934. Dorothy passed away in 1997 and Thee passed away in 2014, outliving his wife and both his daughters.

Mike Keros' other son George Keros volunteered for the military in WWII. He was Killed In Action at Iwo Jima and left behind a wife and children.

230 Galisteo Street in 1938 was occupied by the Handy Way Fruit Market, John Hagidakis (Hadis, Hagis), proprietor. He must have learned the trade from his previous employment in 1936 down the street at 316 Galisteo at the Santa Fe Fruit Market. In 1940 Hagis opened the Chile King Café at 216 West San Francisco Street. John passed that year.

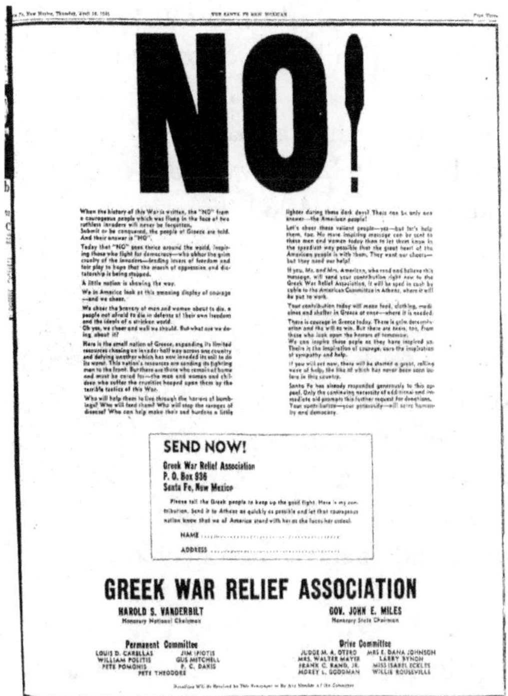

Figure 62. Advertisement for the Greek War Relief Association. *Santa Fe New Mexican*, April 10, 1941.

Here, at the intersection of Galisteo Street and West Alameda Street, we first cross Alameda Street and then we cross the Santa Fe River. This takes us to the 300 block of Galisteo Street. In the 1920's to 1950's there were businesses on the west side of the 300 block of Galisteo Street, and the east side was occupied by the old Governor's Mansion and State buildings.

310 Galisteo Street in 1938 was occupied by the Yucca Café, later the Yucca Bar. Antonio (wife Jeanette) Andreakis (Andreadis) was proprietor of the Yucca Café and Bar from 1938 to his death in 1952. Andreakis was born in 1893 in Greece and enlisted with the U.S. Army in WWI where he served as a cook. He later worked in Walsenburg, Colorado as a miner. He and his wife Jeanette moved to Santa Fe in 1938. They had one son, George Anthony Andreakis, and a daughter, Elaine. George was a popular actor in Walsenburg and in Santa Fe. George enlisted in the Army Air Corps in WWII and his death in late 1945 was listed as DNB or died non-battle. Elaine worked during WWII as clerk at Bruns General (Army) Hospital in Santa Fe. Antonio was a member of the American Legion, the 40&8, and Veterans of Foreign Wars, and was buried at the National Cemetery in Santa Fe. Andreakis had two cousins in Santa Fe: Pete Dakis who operated La Mariposa Bar at 203 West San Francisco Street; and John Hagidakis (Hagis) who operated the Handy Way Fruit Market at 230 Galisteo in 1936 and the Chile King Café at 216 West San Francisco Street in 1940.

By 1947 Andreakis took Louis Zagaris (Zangaris) as partner. Zagaris had worked as a clerk at the Recreation Club in 1938. He was born in 1889 in Greece, was naturalized by 1940, and passed in 1969. He came to Santa Fe from Muhlenberg, Huerfano County, Colorado, where he probably worked as a miner.

316 Galisteo Street from 1936-1938 was the site of the Santa Fe Fruit Market (Figs. 63, 64), a grocery store, owned and operated by Ted Otero (wife Neil) and Dan Razatos. The business lasted through 1938. Afterwards, from November 1938 through at least 1942, Dan Razatos owned and operated the California Fruit Market at 244 Water Street at the corner of Agua Fria. In 1940, Ted Otero owned and operated La Villa Court at 320 Galisteo.

In 1940, the former site of the Santa Fe Fruit Market at 314-316 Galisteo was now Batrite Food Stores (Fig. 65) and Batrite Pastry Shop. Batrite eventually had three stores in Santa Fe and one in Los Alamos.

SANTA FE FRUIT MARKET

316 Galisteo — Phone 162

Opposite Mansion

Folks, we will be closed after Sunday, Nov. 20th to allow the contractors to completely remodel and enlarge the Santa Fe Fruit Market into one of the finest and most convenient places of business in town. We wish to sincerely thank all of our good patrons and customers who have made our phenomenal growth possible and we hasten to assure you all that we always will be in step with progress. Always the very best in the market. Watch for our opening.

Many Thanks.

TED OTERO
DAN RAZATOS

We Are Disposing Of Our Remainig Stock Saturday At Cost

Figure 63.
Advertisement for the Santa Fe Fruit Market.
Santa Fe New Mexican, Nov. 19, 1937.

Figure 64. Advertisement for the Santa Fe Fruit Market. *Santa Fe New Mexican*, Dec. 30, 1937.

THE NEW MEXICAN — Page Seven

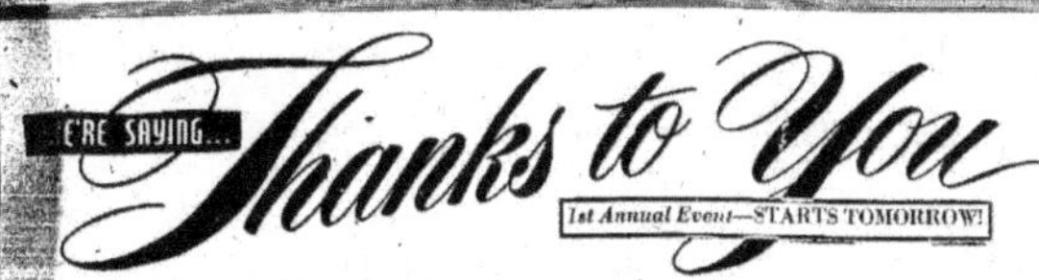

Naturally, as any business firm does, we value . . . and value highly . . . our customers. As a token of our appreciation to you, all four Batrite Food Stores join in bringing you the First Annual Batrite "Gift Time." There's nothing to buy; no skull-cracking rhymes to complete. Simply register at any Batrite Food Store . . . as many times as you like during the four weeks of Batrite's "GIFT TIME."

It's . . . GIFT TIME at all 4 . . . BATRITE FOOD STORES

Dozens of FREE and Valuable GIFTS . . . Awards Every Week for 4 Weeks!

Absolutely Nothing to Buy! Register as Many Times as You Like Each Week at Any BATRITE Food Store!

HERE'S ALL YOU DO:

Stop in at any of the four conveniently located BATRITE FOOD STORES . . . there are three in Santa Fe, one in Los Alamos . . . and register for Batrite's GIFT TIME. That's all you do . . . it's simple . . . it's easy. And you may register just as many times as you like each week during the four weeks that Gift Time will run. There's absolutely nothing to buy . . . no purchase necessary to register. Awards will be made weekly at one of the four *Batrite Food Stores*; according to the schedule at the right. You need not even be present to receive your gift. Watch the New Mexican . . . announcement of those receiving gifts will be made in Batrite Food Stores' regular advertisements. Contest is open to all; of all ages . . . except, of course, employes of the Batrite Food Stores and The New Mexican.

A Free Bicycle EVERY WEEK!

PLUS OTHER VALUABLE GIFTS . . . EACH WEEK!

Gifts Will Be Awarded As Follows at 7 P.M. Each Saturday:

Dec. 1 -Batrite No. 1-120 Lincoln Avenue
Dec. 8 -Batrite No. 4-Western Area LOS ALAMOS (Awards at 6 p. m.)
Dec. 15-Batrite No. 2-316 Galisteo Street
Dec. 22-Batrite No. 3-Cerrillos & Pen Rds.

Register Now! You Need Not Be Present To Receive A Gift!

GIFTS

Are Now On Display
At All Four
BATRITE Food Stores
See Them Now!

Figure 65. Advertisement for Batrite.
The *Santa Fe New Mexican*, Nov. 25, 1951.

324 Galisteo Street was occupied by Mutt & Jeff's Café (Fig. 66), owned and operated from 1934 to 1938 by Gust Razatos. Razatos had previously owned the Liberty Café up the street from 1928-1929.

In 1936, Evangelo Karchiotes joined as partner and Thomas Crusos joined as manager and as cook. By 1940, Karchiotes no longer appeared in the City Directory and the cafe was now owned by Thomas Crusos and Nicholas (Nick) K. Alexander. They ran the cafe until 1942.

By 1944 Crusos was no longer in the City Directory and the cafe was run only by Nick Alexander. In 1947, Nick Alexander was still in the City Directory but Mutt & Jeff's was replaced by Stewart's Restaurant. Nick Alexander was born in 1898 in Greece. He came to Santa Fe around 1940 from Chicago and he was divorced at that time. Nick had a brother Gregory in Santa Fe who passed in 1951 and is buried at Fairview Cemetery. Nick was a member of the American Legion and the Forty and Eight. Like many other Greeks in Santa Fe at the time, Nick participated in a campaign for cigarettes for overseas soldiers and in a War Bond auction. Nick retired by 1948.

In 1934, James Pappas was listed as a cook at Mutt & Jeff's and in 1940 he was listed as a cook at La Bajada Café on Cerrillos Road.

Pete Panagioutou worked at the Mutt & Jeff's Café from 1936 to 1938, as a helper and as a cook.

This address marks the end of our walk down Galisteo Street.

Figure 66. Advertisement for Mutt & Jeff's Café. *Santa Fe New Mexican*, September 1, 1944.

7
WEST WATER STREET

We now backtrack north up Galisteo Street to the intersection with West Water Street, which we previously passed as we crossed from the 100 block to the 200 block of Galisteo Street.

An important landmark on Water Street is Don Gaspar Avenue, which divides Water Street into East and West (Map 6, Fig. 67). The 100 block of West Water Street extends from Don Gaspar Avenue to Galisteo Street. The 200 block of West Water Street extends from Galisteo Street to Sandoval Street.

125 West Water Street was occupied by the Savoy Café (1936–1948) and the Savoy Cocktail Lounge (1948-1953), owned and operated by Michael (wife Alexandra or Alexandria) Kartas (Kariat) (Fig. 68). The cafe was located across the street from the old bus depot at 126 West Water Street.

Mike Kartas appeared in the 1930 U.S. Census in Walsenburg, Colorado. He was born in 1884 in Greece and immigrated in 1909. He was married to Alexandria, who was born in 1899 in Greece and immigrated in 1921. They appeared with four children: Helen (from a previous relationship), Esther, Tony, and Paul. Kartas appeared in the 1932 Santa Fe City Directory as proprietor of the Coney Island Café on 212 West San Francisco Street. In 1934 he was a cook at an unnamed cafe. In 1936 he was listed as a cook at the U&I Café. In 1937 he and William Syrios apparently bought the Savoy Café from Tony Mitchell. In 1948, the café was turned into the Savoy Cocktail Lounge. Mike passed away in 1951. Alexandria kept the cocktail lounge until at least 1953.

In 1947, Gus Baltos was listed as a cook at the Savoy. In 1950 he was a fry cook at the Plaza Café. He was born in 1905 in Greece, never married, and passed in 1956.
Around 1952, Mike George Mellas was said to have lived on the premises of the Savoy. He was born in 1892 in Greece and passed in 1961. His wife Caroline Vigil passed in 1936.

244 West Water Street was occupied from 1942 by the Famous Coney Island (not to be confused with the Coney Island Café on San Francisco Street which closed two years earlier in 1940). The proprietors were not Greek but Gus Poulos worked there as a cook in 1947. Poulos also worked at the Plaza Café as a waiter in 1953.

This takes us to the intersection with Don Gaspar Avenue.

W. SAN FRANCISCO ST.

E. SAN FRANCISCO ST.

100-102 W SF St–
Santa Fe Book &
Stationery

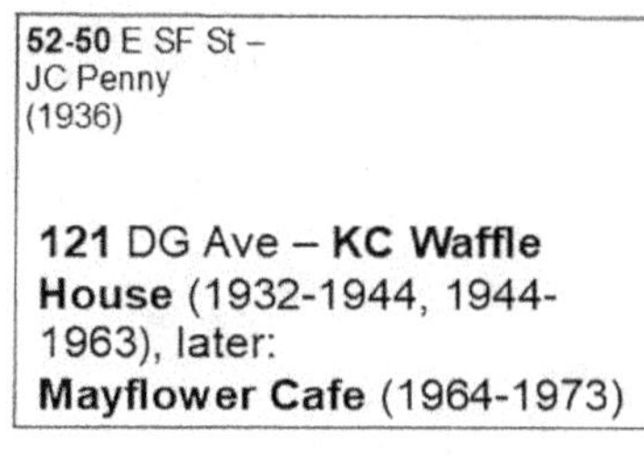

125 W. Water –
Savoy Cafe /
Cocktail Lounge
(1936-1953)

120 DG–
Montezuma
Hotel

DON GASPAR AVE.

W. Water St.

E. Water St.

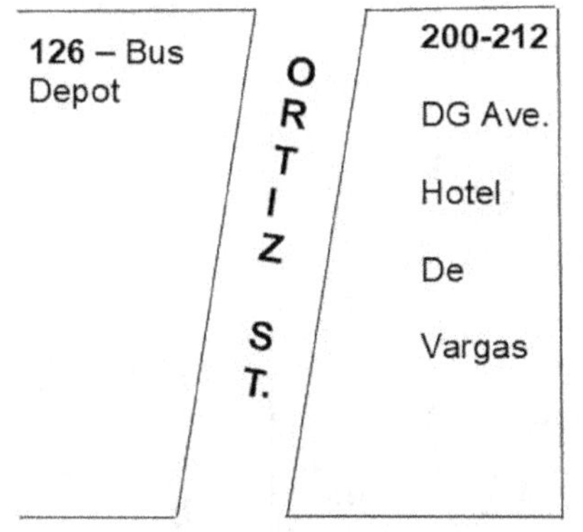

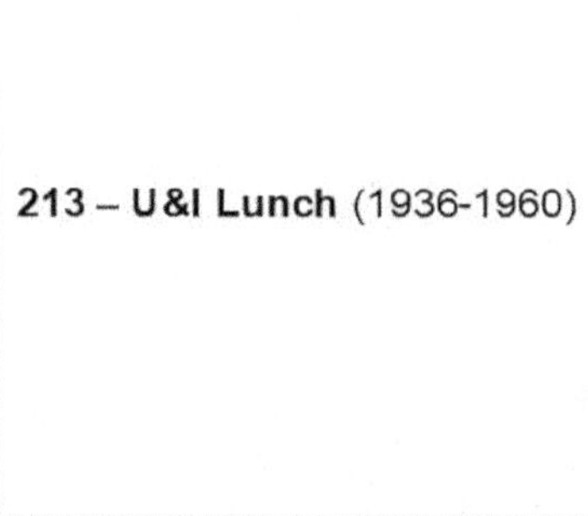

W. ALAMEDA ST.

E. ALAMEDA ST.

SANTA FE
RIVER

SANTA FE
RIVER

Legend:
Names of
Greek-owned
businesses
in **bold**.

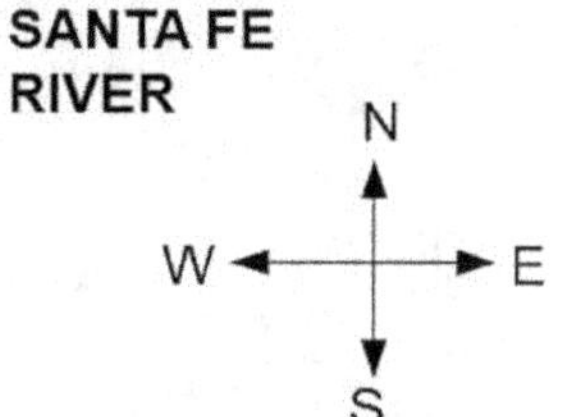

Map 6. Water Street.
This is the same map we use for Don Gaspar Avenue.

Treat Your Credit As A Sacred Trust

L. F. SHELDON & CO.
Retail Merchants Credit Ass'n
CREDITS and COLLECTIONS
17 Blatt Bldg. Phones 422 and 519

337

WASHINGTON AV—(Cont'd)
325 Christensen M F
334 Gable T P ◎
339 Shell A H
341 Gilliland T S
343 Vacant
Kearney av bg es
403 Barton J B
412 Vacant
413 Barrows E L ◎
415 Staplin Frank ◎
417 Bingham Jno
Artist bg es
500 Vacant
500½ High Sch Ath Field
Hettis Way bg es
508 Sprague M H
510 Candelario J S
ws Neumann D L ◎

WATER EAST
Begins 201 Don Gaspar av ext east (Right Even)
105-7 New Method Clnrs
109 Prokosch Elec Co
111 Vacant
113 Tony's Super Tire Serv
119-21 Auto Transit & T Co
123 Underwood-Elliott-Fisher Co
N M Photo Copy Co
Goldenberg C N eng
Ward Carmen Mrs monuments
van Hecke Wiley ins
125 Capitol Auto Sup Co
127 Santa Fe Holding Co
Stamm Allen contr
129 Morris Motor Serv
132 Clarkson Hunter tours
Shelby intersects
200-2 Clarkson Hunter tours
College intersects
223 K of C Hall
223-25-27 St Francis Parochial School
228 Loretto Academy
Cathedral pl intersects

WATER WEST
Begins 200 Don Gaspar av ext west (Right Odd)
125 Savoy Cafe
Ortiz bg ss
126 Manker's Auto Serv
Union Bus Depot
Santa Fe Trailways
Southwestern Greyhound Lines
Inter-City Transit Lines
N M Transp Co
Chama Valley Lines
127 Vacant
128 Central Serv Sta
129 Goodrich Silvertown Stores
131 Zia Service
133 Capital Cab Co
Galisteo intersects
203 Cooney Peter barber
205 Vacant
207 Vacant
211 Pat's Four Four Taxi
215 Nelson Motor Serv
Gelvin-MacAluso Pontiac Co
218 Izard Bros Tire Store
219 Bishop O R 2d hnd gds
220 Candelario Camp
223 Santa Fe Hay & Grain Co
224 Hohman F J & Co contrs
225 Martinez Felipita Mrs
228 Owl Bar
228 Model Cleaners
228½ Murray C E
236 Coors Tavern
242 Quintana B & Co gro
244 Farmers Mkt
246 Calif Frt Mkt
Agua Fria bg ss
300-12 Purdy's Bakery
307 Creamery Del Rico
309 Master Dri-Sheen Clnrs
309½ Irish E E
314-16 County Welfare Dept
315 Coronado Serv Sta
318 Santa Fe Wreck Co
318½ Beevers J F
320 Garcia Catalina Mrs
322 Romero Presciliano
323-33 Santa Fe Elec Lndry
Jefferson intersects
409 Bindel W E
413 Vacant
452 Mac's Feed Store
468 Indep Fuel & Feed Co
480 Sandoval F G
De Fouri ends ss
501 Grill Mill & Carp Shop

WEBBER
Begins 200 E Manhattan ext south (Right Even)
501 Artiaga Delphine
507 Koury M D ◎
511 Myers Alfred
511½ Moore M G Mrs
512 Digneo Chas ◎
513 Rodgers H R
Santa Fe av intersects
611 Robert J B
613 Shaffer Irene Mrs
615 Burns Marion
619 Brownlee J E ◎
629 Floyd V L
629½ Adams H R
631 Vacant
633 Turley W G ◎
Booth ends ws
649 Sanford Alice Mrs

Expert Beauty Service by Competent and Careful Operators

DE VARGAS BEAUTY SHOP

LILAH BROWN
Prop.

PHONE
745

210
Don Gaspar

Figure 67. Page from Hudspeth's 1940 Santa Fe City Directory showing the businesses on Water Street.

ANNOUNCING

The Opening of the

Newly Remodeled

SAVOY

COCKTAIL LOUNGE

125 W. Water St.

We've had a group of experts remodel the inside and outside of the old Savoy Cafe . . . and they have done such a good job streamlining it into the new Savoy Cocktail Lounge that we think you will honestly say

"It's something beautifully different for the City Different."

★ SNAPPY SNACKS

★ FINEST MIXED DRINKS

★ PACKAGED LIQUORS

★ UNEXCELLED SERVICE

"The Place to Go in Santa Fe"
REFINED ATMOSPHERE WITH YOUR FAVORITE DRINKS SERVED BY MIXMASTER PAUL

Savoy Cocktail Lounge

"That New Look"

125 W. Water St.

Figure 68.
Advertisement for Savoy Cocktail Lounge.
Santa Fe New Mexican, Feb. 3, 1948.

DON GASPAR AVENUE

8

DON GASPAR AVENUE

This 100 block of Don Gaspar Avenue extends north-south from San Francisco Street to Water Street and it divides both streets into east and west sections (Map 7, Fig. 69). The 200 block of Don Gaspar Avenue extends from Water Street to Alameda Street. Like Water Street, Don Gaspar Avenue divides Alameda Street into east and west sections.

121 Don Gaspar Avenue at the corner of Don Gaspar Avenue and Water Street in 1928 was the Brown Bobby Coffee Shop owned by two non-Greek women. In 1930 it was Our Way Sandwich Chili Shop. From 1932 to 1944 it was the Kansas City (KC) Waffle House (Shop) (Fig. 70) owned by Gus (wife Sally) T. Mitchell (Fig. 71). By 1947, the KC Waffle House was owned by E. E. Rudolph, and Mitchell was proprietor of Mitchell's Music Store at 205 West San Francisco.

In 1936, Stefano (wife Rhea or Reynalda) Koulroulous was listed as chef at the KC. Koulroulous reappeared in the 1938 and 1940 Santa Fe City Directories (and the 1940 U.S. Census) as Steve J. (wife Reynalda or Rhea) Koutroulis. Koutroulis had married Reynalda Alvord in 1934. Koutroulis passed in 1944.

In 1936, Pete (wife Mathilde) Kopanos was a cook at the KC, but in 1938 he was at the El Fidel Grill and in 1940 he was at the Burro Alley Café.

In 1964, the same address, 121 Don Gaspar Avenue, became the Mayflower Café (Fig. 72) owned by Robert and Georgia (Maryol, a Greek) Gundrey. This establishment had nothing to do with the earlier Mayflower Café on the Plaza, 1930-1955. In 1976, Georgia opened Tomasita's Mexican Kitchen at 1115 Hickox.

We now cross Water Street to reach the 200 block of Don Gaspar. On your left or the southeast corner is the New Mexico Power Company where we would go and pay our electric bill. It is now a parking lot.

Next to the Power Company and across the street from the Hotel De Vargas, at 213 Don Gaspar Avenue, in 1928 was Antonio Windsor's office (a contractor and builder), and the Auto Transit Company, and Guy's Transfer. By 1930, Guy's Transfer was no longer there. By 1934, it was still Antonio Windsor's office, but it also was home to the U&I Lunch (Fig. 73) owned by R. F. Campbell. In 1936, the U&I was owned by Basilios Ioannis Syrios; in 1938 by Jason Mazos; in 1940 by Christos or Chris P. (wife Meda Lee or Medshu, born in 1910 in Oklahoma and passed in Bernalillo County in 1985) Fettas (Fettos, born in 1893 in Greece and passed in Truth or Consequences in 1984); in 1942 by James Sitsas; in 1944 by Antonio Micopoulos; and in 1947 by Tony (wife Bertha) Mitchell. Tony Mitchell owned the U&I at least through 1960. Tony Mitchell had also owned the Savoy Café on Water Street and sold it to William Syrios and Mike Kartas in 1937.

In 1938, Jerry Angelos (Gerasimos Antzoulatos) was listed as a cook at the U&I. Angelos was born in Aprogeraka, Cephalonia in 1889. He immigrated in 1914 and petitioned for citizenship in 1943. From 1949 to 1951 he was a clerk at the Handy Way Liquor.

In 1944, Jason Karagunis was listed as a waiter at the U&I Café.

Basilios Ioannis Syrios, the owner of the U&I in 1936, was born in Granitza, Greece in 1883. He immigrated in 1903. He applied for naturalization in Santa Fe in 1940 and listed himself as single. From 1937 to 1944 he co-owned the Savoy Café with Mike Kartas. In 1944 he was also a clerk at the Plaza Hotel (but he did not live there) and he had a son William Jr. In 1947 Basilios was a telephone operator.

James Sitsas, owner of the U&I in 1942, was born in 1891 in Greece. In the 1940 U.S. Census in Santa Fe he was listed as divorced and working as a cook. He passed in 1942.

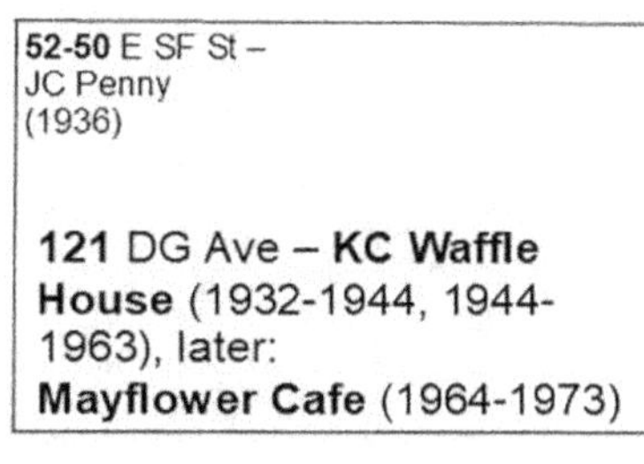

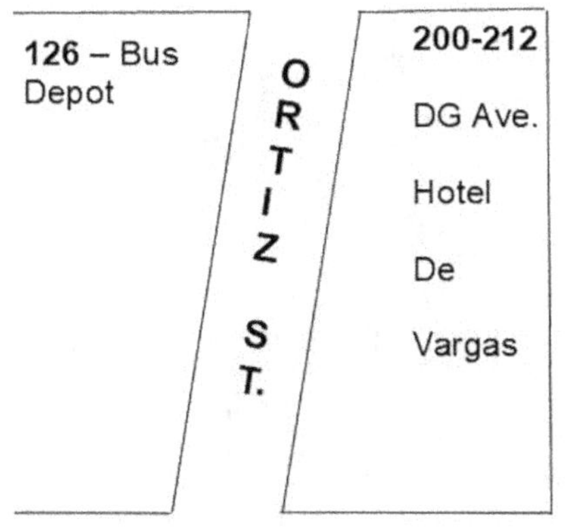

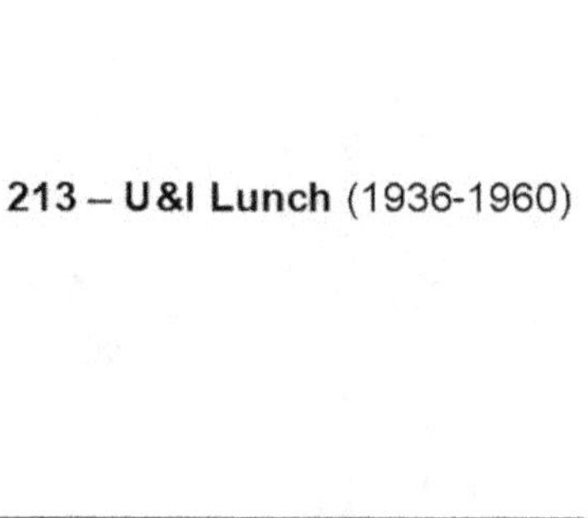

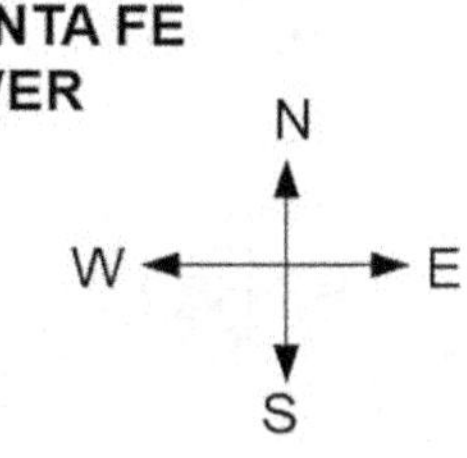

Map 7. Don Gaspar Avenue.

CANDELARIO FINANCE CO.

LOANS — INVESTMENTS — REAL ESTATE — INSURANCE

138 W. Palace Ave. **Phone 2044**

308

What do you do with the Old Directory?

You may need to keep it in your file for the purpose of getting antecedent information about new customers and to relocate old ones through former employers and neighbors. Otherwise take the old book home where it will be as great a convenience as at the office it was a business asset.

DON DIEGO—(Cont'd)

742 Sweeney R P ◎

W Buena Vista av intersects

811 Lewis J W ◎
815 Hagner H H ◎
823 Ludwick I L
833 Bennett R W ◎
837 Rogers C J ◎
838 Goodwin A B
840 Smith W C
841 Lucero B E Mrs ◎
849 Vacant
rear Orr O O ◎
851 Hyde C A ◎
rear Ingalls F G
853 Vacant
864 Romero M L ◎
865 Kahre A H ◎
1018 Rubenstein Louis
1020 Cudabac H M
1022 Cantu A M ◎
1027 Grimes Celia ◎
1027½ Byrne Verne
1028 Kirk S L ◎
1032 Garrett W R
1034 Crowe G A
1036 Sebastian V G

DON FELIX

Begins after 206 Closson ext west (Right Odd)

615 Roybal Amado ◎
616 Winer Gus
617 Urban Placido ◎
618 Gonzalez Leo ◎

Casados bg ss

621 Gonzalez L A ◎
624 Napoleon I L Mrs ◎
625 Espinosa J D
630 Gonzalez C B ◎
631 Thayer F W ◎

Barela ends ns
Irvine bg

702 Melendez Alfonso ◎
703 Romero L L ◎
708 Sandoval L J ◎
709 Beachel E B ◎
713 Martinez J M ◎

DON GASPAR AV

Begins 100 W San Francisco is the principal street running south and is the point from which numbers on the intersecting streets begin (Right Even)

110 Old Mexico Shop curios
112 Parkhurst Studio
114-16 Feldhake Mac Foowear
115 Ortiz Bros jwlrs
116 Schramm Cliff wtchmkr
116½ La Von Beauty Shop
117 Alarid H C shoemkr
120 Montezuma Hotel
121 K C Waffle House

Water intersects

se cor New Mexico Power Co
200-12 Hotel De Vargas
De Vargas Drug Co
De Vargas Dispensary
De Vargas Barber Shop
De Vargas Beauty Shop
De Vargas Coffee Shop
De Vargas Bar
De Vargas News Stand
213 U & I Cafe
216-18 St John's M E Church
225-27 Don Carlos Motor Co
228 Burro Weavers
Santa Fe Handwoven Fabrics
230 Western Auto Sup Co
231 N M Text Book Dep
232 Motor Equip Co
233 Superior Baking Co
234-38 Closson & Closson autos
Standard Oil Co
235 Acme Auto Serv

Alameda bg es

es N M Supreme Court Bldg

De Vargas intersects

301 Laughlin K K Mrs ◎

N Capitol bg ws

329 Morgan I L
333 Sanchez L F ◎
337 Lutz H S ◎
341 Grissom R H
343 Balling F C
347a Shepard Guy
347b Van Leer R J
347c Melaven Jack
347d Newman J R

S Capitol bg ws

402 McGill R S Mrs
403 Taichert D H ◎
406 Douthirt C H
407 Dendahl Henry ◎
410 Worden G F
414 Kahn Gus
416 Wheeler L E
420 Stinson Anne Mrs
427 Gallinger Rolph
nw cor First Bapist Church

Manhattan intersects

505 Salmon Nathan ◎
508 Pauly N J
510 Brooks I C Mrs
515 Fiske J F Mrs ◎
516 Brown C E
518 Ervien Sibyl Mrs
524 Gallegos J C
527 Garcia J O ◎
528 Neel G M ◎
532 McCauley J O ◎

Santa Fe av intersects

603 Thomason Betty
605 Dyer C R
607 Yoder H B

Figure 69. Page from Hudspeth's 1940 Santa Fe City Directory.

Figure 70.
Advertisement for the KC Waffle House.
Santa Fe New Mexican, August 31, 1945.

Figure 71. From left front moving counterclockwise: Harry Dakos (dark suit), Art Maringas (white shirt), Helen Pomonis at far head of table, Sarando "Ike" Kalangis, Sally and Gus Mitchell, Tom Pomonis at near head of table. Photo in author's collection.

BEST FOOD!
BEST SERVICE!
THE MOST
POPULAR PRICES!
American and Mexican
Dishes!
MAYFLOWER
CAFE
Corner Don Gaspar-Water St.

Figure 72. Advertisement for the Mayflower Café on Don Gaspar Avenue *Santa Fe New Mexican*, July 11, 1966.

TO OUR FRIENDS

May your every
wish be granted,
every hour filled
with happiness, and
good cheer be yours
at Christmas
and throughout the
new year ahead.

U & I
LUNCH

Figure 73. Advertisement for the U&I Lunch.
Santa Fe New Mexican, Dec. 24, 1945.

AGUA FRIA

9
AGUA FRIA

Starting with this chapter, we cover outliers from the downtown.

308 Hancock (the street no longer exists) was occupied in 1936 by the Quality Bakery, John Xurekes (Hurekes, Zurekes) and Nick Bagonis (Pagones), proprietors. By 1938, the business was moved to 223 West Montezuma Avenue (Fig. 74), Xurekes was sole proprietor, and Bagonis (Pagones) was listed as a cook at an unnamed cafe. Later that same year, in August 1938, a notice appeared in the *Santa Fe New Mexican* that Gust Prappas [sic] was now the owner and operator of the Quality Bakery. In 1940, Pappas and the Quality Bakery were no longer listed, and Xurekes was listed as owning the Home Bakery (Fig. 75) at 612 Agua Fria Street. In 1945, Xurekes moved the bakery down the street to 632 Agua Fria. It appeared under new management 12 years later in March 1957 but at the same address, 632 Agua Fria. In the same year, 1957, Xurekes was listed as owning the J Lane Bakery and living at 632 Agua Fria but there was no separate entry for the J Lane Bakery. This was the last City Directory listing for Xurekes. Xurekes was born in 1888 in Greece and never married. All the Greeks in Santa Fe patronized his bakery because his bread was so good!

From 1936-1937, John Apostolakis was a helper at the Quality Bakery. He was admitted in the 1940's to the Greek AHEPA TB Sanatorium in Albuquerque.

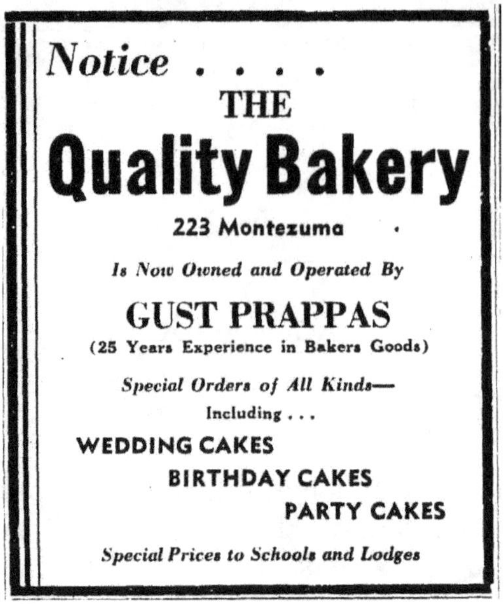

Notice . . . .

THE

Quality Bakery

223 Montezuma

Is Now Owned and Operated By

GUST PRAPPAS

(25 Years Experience in Bakers Goods)

Special Orders of All Kinds—

Including . . .

WEDDING CAKES

BIRTHDAY CAKES

PARTY CAKES

Special Prices to Schools and Lodges

Figure 74.
Advertisement for the Quality Bakery.
Santa Fe New Mexican, August 19, 1938.

The New

HOME BAKERY

632 Agua Fria

Will Be Open

TOMORROW

Figure 75.
Advertisement for the Home Bakery.
Santa Fe New Mexican, Oct. 31, 1945.

10
PALACE AVENUE, COLLEGE STREET, CERRILLOS ROAD, AND BEYOND

In this chapter we will cover the remaining Greeks and Greek businesses in Santa Fe.

Palace Avenue

In 1930, George Mitchell was a chef at the Sena Plaza Restaurant on Palace Avenue near the Plaza and the Cathedral.

College Street

303 College Street in 1936 was the site of the Bar-B-Q Stand. Athan and Gust Meimary were proprietors and were living in the vicinity at Orchard Camp, a set of 65 to 70 cottages ("modern apartments and hotel accomodations") near the northeast corner of East Alameda Street and College Street (now Old Santa Fe Trail) adjacent the Santa Fe River. Orchard Camp was established in 1923 by John Walz Catron, eldest son of U.S. Senator Thomas B. Catron and Julia Walz Catron. Athan passed in 1938 and his funeral was well attended. In 1938, "S." (wife Magdaline) Meimary was proprietor of the Orchard Camp Café. Athan Meimaroglou was born in 1889 in Adramete, Turkey. He immigrated in 1907 through England to Boston and in 1917 he was working as a chef in Springfield, Massachusetts. He declared his intention to naturalize in 1925 when he was single and working as a baker in Detroit, Michigan. He naturalized in 1926 and shortened his last name to Meimary. In 1931 in Holbrook, Arizona he married Elinor Cotter, Jim Ipiotis and Michael Hatze, witnesses. Soterios Meimary (wife Magdaline) later reappears in 1947 to 1960 in Michigan.

Cerrillos Road

From 1936 to 1944, Steve (wife Maria Savina Rael or Mary or Lola) Coukas ran the Indian Grocery Store (which was also a restaurant) on Tesuque Drive across from the Santa Fe Indian School. By 1947 he was running the Home Dispensary liquor store at 632 1/2 Agua Fria. He was born in 1892 in Greece, was naturalized, and passed in 1969. Mary his wife was born in 1904 and passed in 1981.

In 1940, Nick Dantis (Dantist), owned and operated the La Bajada Café near Navajo Blvd. He was born Nicholaos Tantidakis in 1893, immigrated in 1909, and changed his name at naturalization in 1934 while working as a miner in McKinley County, New Mexico. By the 1950 U.S. Census he was married to Beninga of Santa Fe and had four children.

John (wife Irene) Pappas was listed in 1940 as a cook at the La Bajada Café. Previously in 1934 he was listed as a cook at Mutt & Jeff's.

Peter or Panos (wife Nona Mae) B. Anastas or Anastos in 1938 to 1940 was proprietor of the Nona Mae Café on Cerrillos Rd. and then apparently moved back to Texas. Peter was born in 1894 in Macedonia. He was in the United States during WWI and registered to serve in the U.S. Armed Forces. He had previously been in Witchita Falls, Texas, from at least 1929 to 1935, where his wife was from. They had one son. His wife Nona Mae passed in 1950. After the move to Texas we lose track of Peter. Also working at the café as a cook was Pete's brother Sam A. Anastas, married to Edna from Missouri.

In 1932, Pete Rigas had the Trail Pig Stand Café on Cerrillos Rd. Earlier, from 1923 to 1928, he had been a proprietor of the Santa Fe Chocolate Shop at 60 East San Francisco Street.

In 1932, Charles Hermes worked at the Trail Pig Stand Café as a cook. In 1934, Hermes and John Xurekes (Zurekes) apparently bought the cafe from Rigas. The cafe was closed by 1936. From 1936 to 1938 Hermes was a cook at the Laguna Café on Galisteo Street and married to Margarita Benevidez. Hermes eventually moved into retail management and was in Santa Fe at least through 1949. In 1936, Xurekes opened the Quality Bakery with Nick Bagonis (Pagones), as discussed in Chapter 9.

Tom Pomonis opened the Cerrillos Liquor Store in 1952 after retiring from the Mayflower Café on the Plaza.

Manuel or Mannie (wife Nancy) Gianopoulos was a bartender at the Plaza Cocktail Lounge in 1951. In 1953 he owned A&M Bar & Dispensary on Cerrillos Road with Alex Kalangis, and owned Manny's Cocktail Lounge from 1955 to 1959 on Cerrillos Road. Manny was born in 1916 in Maine. His wife was born in 1925 in Kallone, Lesbos, Greece. He passed in 1995 and she passed in 2016.

Pete Lelekas was married to Lizzie who owned the Kiva Inn on Cerrillos Road. They appeared only in the 1936 Santa Fe City Directory. Otherwise, he appeared in Gallup City Directories in the 1950's.

Other Locations

100 West Barcelona Street was the site of the piano studio of Sara F. Evangelides. She was not Greek herself.

I now discuss Greeks who were listed by profession or address but not by business or employer. I begin with the Santa Fe City Directories, and then turn to the U.S. Census in Santa Fe.

In the Santa Fe City Directories:

Basil D. Lampros was born in 1888 in Greece. He first appeared in the Santa Fe Newspaper in 1943 as MC at a dinner for overseas men at Eppie's Café. In the late 1950's he appeared as President of Cristino Rivera Mining Corporation. He passed in 1962.

Steve (wife Candelaria) Koroneos first appeared in the 1938 Santa Fe City Directory. The 1940 U.S. Census listed him as an assistant cook. It also listed his wife and their six children. Steve was born in 1886 in Greece and passed in 1967. Candelaria was born in 1904 in New Mexico and passed in 1991.

Michael or Mike (wife Emelia or Ema Alexander) Speratos (Sparatos, Spiratos) had five children. Their son Jerry enlisted in the U.S. Marines in 1940 and served at Pearl Harbor. They were in Santa Fe in 1938 living on Navajo Blvd so it is possible that Mike worked at La Bajada Café. They moved to Escondido, California. Mike was born around 1893 and passed in 1972.

In the 1930 U.S. Census in Santa Fe:

Jim Karamonzio (DC Karamonzis), born around 1900 and immigrated in 1922, was listed in the 1930 U.S. Census in Santa Fe as a waiter and in the 1932 Santa Fe City Directory as a cook.

John Giannario, born in 1903, was listed as naturalized, working as a cook, and living at the Plaza Hotel.

Daniel Ronlous (?), born in 1907, worked as a shoemaker, and shared his home at 240 Washington Avenue with his widowed sister, Konstantina Spelestopoulas, ten years his senior.

In the 1940 U.S. Census in Santa Fe:

In the 1940 U.S. Census, Steve Goodas, age 54, was a cook working on his own account, naturalized, and living with Annie Goodas, age 24.

In the 1940 U.S. Census, there appeared a John Charania (Chavarias or Chavarria). He was born around 1895 in Greece, was naturalized and owner of a "public cafe."

In 1949, Peter Tzeranis was a grocer.

Pete Panaguton was listed as living in Lordsburg, New Mexico and working as a cook, but having lived in Santa Fe in 1935.

Tony Charnas was listed as living in Ranchos de Albuquerque, New Mexico and was naturalized, but having lived in Santa Fe in 1935.

Thomas Bobas was listed as living in Los Angeles, working as a dishwasher, an alien, and possibly married, but having lived in Santa Fe in 1935.

James Vosoras was listed as living in Tucson, Arizona, widowed, having applied for naturalization, working in private work, but having lived in Santa Fe in 1935.

Isaak Columbus was listed as living in St. Paul, Minnesota, married, naturalized, and working as a cook, but having lived in Santa Fe in 1935.

In the 1950 U.S. Census in Santa Fe:

George (wife Betty from Kansas) Stamoulis, born in Greece in 1913 to Constantin Stamoulis and Ellen P Papademetrio, was an electrician. He and his wife also appeared in the 1947 and 1949 Santa Fe City Directories. Also appearing in the 1950 U.S. Census was Cleo Harris, discussed below, whose mother was Helen Stamoulis. These two men, George Stamoulis and Cleo Harris, might have been related. Just remember there were many men coming into the area during the war to work at Los Alamos.

Tom Castriti, born in Greece in 1901, was a cook working at an unnamed restaurant and living at the El Fidel Hotel. He was divorced and came from Charlottesville, Virgina.

George M. Christy was a choir cantor and his wife Lucille was a teacher at the Santa Fe Indian School.

Lester (wife Georgia) Philips owned a liquor store.

Nick Chelimides was a clerk at the Ship Ahoy Liquor Store.

Pete (wife Georgia) Mavropoulose, son Angelo, was a cook at an unnamed restaurant.

Gus Karos worked as a cashier at a restaurant. He appeared in the 1950 U.S. Census in Santa Fe and in the 1960 Santa Fe City Directory. He was born in 1894 and passed in Michigan in 1965.

Jim Jargunes appeared only in the 1950 U.S. Census. Age 73, married, he lived alone at 210 De Vargas.

Guss Themas, not working at age 57, shared a house with Mike Torakis at 223 ½ Montezuma. He was likely the same as Sam Themas who appeared in the 1930 U.S. Census in Savanna, Illinois. He immigrated in 1917, naturalized, was a widower, and had worked as a railroad section foreman. He had three sons and a daughter.

Cleo Harris, not working at age 61, lived alone at 435 Galisteo Street. He was born in 1890 in Greece to Argyrios Hadoulis and Hellen Stamoulis. In the 1930 U.S. Census he was living in Cincinnati, Ohio, was single, naturalized, and working as a mechanical engineer in the automobile industry. In the 1940 U.S. Census he was working in Kalamazoo, Michigan.

Constantine Pavlou, not working at age 62, lived alone at 435 Galisteo Street.

Andy Dovas, age 57, worked as a manager of a bar and shared a house with George Virzoki, a bartender, at 437 Galisteo Street.

George Kostolias, age 56, worked as a cook and shared a house at 306 West Manhattan with Andy Anitsakis.

Mike Kaldo, age 66, was a cook. He shared a house at 137 East De Vargas with Tom Yanatos, Dennis (Dan) Vorres, and three non-Greeks.

Steve (wife Candelaria) Karonesa, age 60, was unemployed, and lived at 55 ½ Tarcido with his wife and their five children.

Jerry (wife Precilla from Kansas) Mintos (Minetos), age 42, worked as a restaurant manager, and lived at 2620 Cerrillos Road with his wife and daughter and sister-in-law.

11
CONCLUSION

This has been the story of the first Greeks of Santa Fe, 1914 to 1955. Many of the people mentioned in this book came from humble origins, from nineteenth-century villages in rural Greece or Turkey. Many came over legally, while others stowed away, but most eventually gained U.S. citizenship, some through military service. They initially brought with them only a very small amount of money, but they all possessed an invaluable work ethic through which they contributed to their new community and to their new country. The first Greeks of Santa Fe opened businesses, raised families, and bought war bonds. Some served in the United States armed forces and some made the ultimate sacrifice. Though I did not talk about it here, some of the children of these first Greeks of Santa Fe stayed in business, while others chose higher education and became academics or professionals. We of the first two generations have a great deal of pride in what we and our parents accomplished and how we contributed a new chapter to the multi-ethnic, multi-cultural story that is Santa Fe. Viva la ciudad diferente!

So, what did I learn from all of this research? As a young girl, I had heard that the Greeks were always changing businesses. "Oh, now he's there," with eyes rolling. At the time I didn't appreciate or understand what they meant. Now I do! Through the years I have shared some of these stories with my son Yorgos who co-authored this book with me, just as many Greek parents proudly shared their stories with their children. The Greek-American story in Santa Fe is a story of entrepreneurship. Greeks bought into and sold businesses, some non-Greek-owned and some Greek-owned, with alarming alacrity! They went from fruit markets to restaurants, from candy stores to sandwich shops to bars. They owned one business while working for another. They were industrious, inventive, tenacious, and ambitious—all of which are character traits required for an immigrant to become a successful entrepreneur and a self-made man (Fig. 76).

Figure 76.
Brothers Tom and Pete Pomonis, restaurateurs and proprietors of the Mayflower Café on the Plaza. Circa 1941.

www.ingramcontent.com/pod-product-compliance
Lightning Source LLC
LaVergne TN
LVHW010624100826
845148LV00014B/3104

* 9 7 8 1 6 3 2 9 3 6 7 5 2 *